Get Plants

First published in 2017 by the Royal Botanic Gardens,
Kew, Richmond, Surrey, TW9 3AB, UK
www.kew.org

ISBN 978 1 84246 627 8

Distributed on behalf of the Royal Botanic Gardens, Kew in North America by the University of Chicago Press, 1427 East 60th St, Chicago, IL 60637, USA.

British Library Cataloguing in Publication Data
A catalogue record for this book is available from the British Library.

Editorial Development: Anna Mumford and Gina Fullerlove
Copyediting: Jean Postle
Proof reading: Sharon Whitehead
Design and page layout: Michelle Noel, Studio Noel
Production management: Andrew Illes

For information or to purchase all Kew titles please visit shop.kew.org/kewbooksonline or email publishing@kew.org

Kew's mission is to be the global resource in plant and fungal knowledge, and the world's leading botanic garden.

Kew receives about half of its running costs from Government through the Department for Environment, Food and Rural Affairs (Defra). All other funding needed to support Kew's vital work comes from members, foundations, donors and commercial activities, including book sales.

Printed and bound by Gomer Press Limited

By Katherine Price
with photography by Sarah Cuttle

Get Plants

How to bring green into your life

Contents

Foreword 06

Preface 07

Introduction

Why you need plants 09

How to use this book 10

What's in a name? 11

Part One:
What plants need

Fire 15

Water 16

Earth 17

Air 20

Lurve 21

Part Two:
Plants

Dramatic 25

Edible 35

Elegant 45

Trashy 57

Natural 69

Odd 79

Charming 89

Retro 99

Structural 109

Part Three: Places

Great outdoors 121

The yard or town garden 123

Balcony or terrace 135

Doorstep 145

Window boxes and ledges 151

Equally great indoors 161

Tilting at windowsills 163

Macramé central 171

Stairwell to heaven 177

All about the hall 181

Bathroom 187

Kitchen 193

Living room 199

Bedroom 209

Part Four: Buy, care and share

Buy 218

Provenance 219

Care 220

Containers 222

Watering 224

Feeding 226

Potting on 227

Look after your leaves 228

Is there a doctor in the house? 229

Pruning and deadheading 230

Share 232

Take cuttings 234

Appendix 237
Index 239
Acknowledgements 240

Foreword

———

There is a popular but unhelpful misconception that you need to be 'an expert' to grow plants well. Certainly training, experience and timely advice provide a sound basis for being a 'plant person', but so also is a healthy measure of pure trial and error. Everyone starts somewhere with plants, whether young or later in life. Even the most celebrated horticulturists, some of whom have contributed their comments to this book, embarked as novices. The point is that they started. Often it was a particular type of plant that captured their attention – interest, knowledge and success blossomed, fueled by a sense of enquiry.

One of the amazing things about living in the 21st century is that we have access to plants from around the world, from extraordinarily varied environments. They are diverse, and many are highly evolved for success in their natural habitats. It just happens that this also means that many are ideally suited to growing in our domestic niches – be they in a container in a shared flat, on a windowsill or balcony, or in a garden plot.

I hope that through reading and enjoying this wonderful book, many more people will be encouraged to 'have a go' – to be enticed to share their living spaces with plants, to seek to understand their needs, to enjoy the successes, and to learn from minor setbacks. All of our lives are richer when shared with plants!

Richard Barley
Director of Horticulture, Learning & Operations
Royal Botanic Gardens, Kew

Preface

———

I was lucky enough to work for nearly ten years as a gardener at the Royal Botanic Gardens, Kew. It's a special place - a dreamy landscape by the River Thames in southwest London, with stunning glass palaces. Every last bit of space is crammed with plants from around the world, from magnificent trees to tiny alpine flowers and rare tropical orchids – some 35,000 species. But it's also the people that make it extraordinary – horticulturists, scientists and all the other folk who make the place tick. They are united in their work to celebrate and protect the plant kingdom in all its weird and wonderful glory. Dotted throughout this book are quotes from Kew gardeners about plants – the ones they wouldn't be without, the ones that first got them into plants – and their tips for keeping plants healthy and happy. To find out how to keep the plants at Kew in the best possible health, they pay a lot of attention to where they come from in the world. The backstories of the plants featured in this book give an indication of how to look after them. I hope that this book will offer practical help and a bit of inspiration to people starting out on their own adventures with plants.

Introduction

Why you need plants

All life depends on plants. They make your existence possible.

Plants are the great alchemists. They produce oxygen, purify and distribute the planet's water, regulate the climate and are the backbone of all habitats. Plants give you food, medicines, textiles, dyes, containers, shelter, building materials, furniture (I could go on).

So far, so practical. But they also make your life richer.

A stack of research shows that having plants around improves your mood and memory, helping you to concentrate. Studies show that people who spend time with plants have better relationships and that caring for ornamental plants increases your levels of positive energy and helps you feel secure and relaxed.

And looking after these amazing organisms is fun – fun and fascinating and compelling. It just is.

Survival / beauty / wellness / mindfulness / fun

Opposite, long-flowering pincushion flowers will bring bees, butterflies and hoverflies to your balcony all summer

How to use this book

So you want to get plants into your life? Good idea.
Congratulations on being an advanced human being.

This book is not a textbook. Instead, it aims to get you thinking of plants not just as decorations but as living organisms with intriguing back stories. They have evolved over millions of years through super-complex interactions with other plants and animals, and it is these interactions that give them their extraordinary diversity of colour, form, life cycle.

The plants in this book are widely available, straightforward to grow, and worth getting to know. They are individuals, with individual needs and characters. This book will give you ideas about which ones to share your life with.

Get plants – don't just acquire them, understand them.

Part One: What plants need – find out the basics of plant life.

Part Two: Plants – think about how you live and find plants that fit your style, your interests, the rhythm of your days. These pages are packed with stories about where in the world these plants come from and what makes them special and worthy of your care.

Part Three: Places – think about where you live and find plants that fit your living space, inside and outside. These pages are full of ideas for plants that will enjoy the different areas of your home.

Part Four: Buy, care, share – the plants recommended in this book are easy to get hold of and simple to grow. These pages help you to bring green and glorious new friends into your life and keep them there.

What's in a name?

The plants in this book come from all over the world.
They are known by different names from country to country.
Even from region to region.

The wild pansy, from Europe, is also known as heartsease or love-in-idleness. The Swiss cheese plant, which comes from tropical rainforests in the Americas, is also called Mexican breadfruit and ceriman. So, to avoid confusion, the scientific name for the plant is also given. This name – consisting of at least two Latin words – identifies a particular species and means that we can be absolutely sure we're talking about the same thing. There are spider plants and spiderworts – two very different plants, but it's easy to mix up the names. However, *Chlorophytum comosum* is the scientific name for a spider plant, while *Tradescantia fluminensis* is a spiderwort, and these names really can't be mixed up.

Finding out a plant's name can be a challenge – supermarkets often sell plants labelled 'Houseplant', nothing more! It's worth making the effort to find out which plant you've got – a leafy plant from a tropical forest will have very different needs to a succulent from a sunny place. They have different back stories too – and it's always good to know who you're sharing your space with.

Whether you're after the brazen razzmatazz of dahlias, opposite, or the cool trailing tradescantia, above, plants transform places

Part One: What plants need – it's elemental

Look outside. Unless you're really unlucky – or living in a shipping container in the Antarctic – you'll see a plant of some sort. Plants stay in one place – they can't move around to get what they need to survive and thrive, so they source it where they grow.

So what do they need? Nothing less than the four elements – earth (nutrients), air (heat), fire (light) and water. Just like us, in fact. But the amount of each element required varies dramatically from plant to plant, depending on where in the world they have evolved. And even plants from tropical forests have a cycle of growth and dormancy that affects their needs through the year.

Fire

Light is a critical ingredient for healthy plants. Natural light is best – emanating from the sun. Artificial light, unless it has been manufactured especially for plant-growing, lacks some of the wavelengths that plants need.

What do plants do with light? Plants need light for their most famous trick – photosynthesis. Using the green pigment chlorophyll as a catalyst, they harness light energy to synthesise sugar and oxygen from carbon dioxide and water. They use the sugar to power all their bodily functions, including growing, flowering and fruiting.

Imagine you're a plant from a rocky Mediterranean hillside. Trees and shrubs are few and far between and you get sun all day long (on a cloudless day). Your tiny leaves reduce waterloss and your hairy surfaces act as a sunscreen too. By contrast, imagine you're a plant from a tropical forest. High above you is the tree canopy, a dense layer of tree leaves and vines. Below that is the understorey, a layer of saplings, smaller trees and shrubs. Living on the ground, you evolve big leaves to catch what little light reaches the forest floor.

Plants have very different light requirements, depending on the habitat they come from. This is great news for us. Whether we have a shady courtyard or a scorching windowsill, there is a plant that will thrive.

But it's important to get it right. The light levels in your living space and outdoor areas change throughout the day. Get to know the way the light fluctuates, whether your window or doorstep faces north, south, east or west (apart from anything, it's good for improving your home's *feng shui*). Then you'll be able to make best use of the following terms you'll come across again and again throughout the book.

LIGHT LEVELS

Full sun – at least five hours of direct sunlight per day (a south-facing window or wall if you're in the northern hemisphere)

Part sun – two or three hours of direct sunlight and bright indirect light for the rest of the day (an east- or west-facing window or wall; remember, the afternoon sun in the west can be very powerful in summer)

Light shade – bright indirect light without any direct sun (a north-facing window or wall if you're in the northern hemisphere)

Shade – no direct sunlight and low light levels even at midday (but enough natural light to cast a shadow)

'There's nothing worse than putting a sun-loving plant in a shady corner, or a shade-loving plant in full sun! Find out what plants like best and try to keep them happy.'

Richard Wilford, gardens designer, Kew

Opposite, flanked by two cacti, the brightly coloured insect traps of the pitcher plant light up in the sun

Water

All life on Earth needs water. The water cycle is a never-ending process in which water evaporates into the air, becomes part of a cloud, falls down to earth as precipitation, and then evaporates again. Plants play a key role in this cycle, taking up water from the ground and emitting it through their leaves and stems back into the atmosphere in a process known as transpiration.

to its roots and back again. In non-woody plants, the pressure of water in the plants' cells is what keeps them upright. If there's a water shortage, even a very local one in a very particular plant pot, the plant may flop and stop growing.
If this is not remedied, the plant will die.

But hang on. One of the main enemies of container-grown plants is actually too much water. Get the watering right and you're most of the way towards green-fingered nirvana.

For hints and tips on watering, see *Watering* on page 224.

'Get a water butt! They are easy to install and store the rain from your roof. And if you're on a water meter, they will save you money in the long run. Most importantly, be attentive and don't be afraid to make mistakes (such as overwatering), as they can teach you valuable lessons! Learn a little about where your plant comes from, as this will help you give it the conditions it needs.'

Amazingly, a plant is typically around 90 per cent water.

Water is one of the ingredients a plant needs for photosynthesis – the production of sugar. Water transports sugar and nutrients around the plant's structures, from its shoots

Scott Taylor, temperate plants specialist, Kew

Earth

In their natural habitats, the vast majority of plants get all the nutrients they need from the soil. The nutrients are dissolved in water and are taken up by the plants' roots. (Roots also serve to anchor plants and can act as stores for excess food.)

The most important plant nutrients are nitrogen, phosphorus and potassium. Nitrogen supports leafy growth and gives a dark green colour to leaves. Phosphorus encourages the formation of flowers and seeds and helps root growth. It improves a plant's resistance to disease, just like potassium, which also encourages root growth and helps to make chlorophyll.

There are other micro-nutrients that are vital for a plant's health and are taken up in water by plant roots – like a vitamin and mineral health drink! Absorbing certain minerals can be a problem for plants if the soil is too alkaline. And if the soil is dry, the plant suffers not only from lack of water, but also from lack of nutrients.

Find out about *Composts* on page 220.

There are a handful of amazing plants that can't get all they need through their roots and supplement their 'diet' in other ways – see *Bromeliads* on page 28, *Air plants* on page 86 and *Carnivores* on page 80.

Regular watering of containers leaches the nutrients out of the compost, so this needs to be refreshed regularly. Or you can feed your plants. Find out about *Feeding* on page 226.

All garden and houseplants need light, water, heat and nutrients, but some need more than others, depending on their origins around the globe

Air

Most common houseplants come from tropical regions and enjoy the same temperatures we do – around 18–24°C (65–75°F). Most plants grown outdoors in containers are from temperate and subtropical regions, where temperatures in the growing season are in the range of 10–18°C (50–65°F). While they will usually tolerate fluctuations either side of this, they will almost certainly suffer if subjected to blasts of heat and cold.

Keep indoor plants away from fires and radiators and out of the direct stream of cooling vents. Plants that have evolved in habitats that don't experience frost are unlikely to be able to withstand a serious chill. So while many houseplants appreciate a summer holiday outdoors (under the right light conditions), they need to be brought back indoors before temperatures plunge.

Many outdoor plants can tolerate high temperatures and intense sunshine as long as their roots are cool. Plants from temperate regions have evolved strategies to deal with the changing seasons, including ways of avoiding damage by the cold.

Frost causes the water in plant cells to freeze. Water expands as it freezes, rupturing cell walls, and the damage can be fatal. In some plants, falling autumn temperatures trigger the accumulation of sugars and amino acids that act like anti-freeze, lowering the freezing point of cell contents. Frost also locks up the moisture in the soil, so, odd as it may sound, plants can be damaged by drought during a long cold period.

Snow is actually an insulating blanket that protects plants from the cold – many mountain plants from above the tree line survive the harsh winters by ticking along quietly under the snow, waiting for the spring thaw when they can leap into action again. Snow, however, is heavy, and that's what can damage the plants.

Left, evergreen plants from temperate climates can deal with low temperatures, but plants that have evolved in tropical zones will not survive a hard frost

Lurve

I stood next to a woman at a flower show who was buying air plants – each time the nursery owner produced another spiky little plant, she squealed with delight: 'Oh, look at him. I must have him!' She spent a lot of money and by the time she left (with a spring in her step and a grin on her face) – she had already made a relationship with her plants.

One of my cacti is called Mollie after my 87-year-old friend, as its pretty hair-do reminds me of her shampoo-and-set. Furthermore, I have a friend whose Swiss cheese plant is called Cheddar.

You can't help bonding with your plants – you'll remember who gave you that pelargonium cutting or the stall at the village fête where you bought those chilli plants, while the succulent on your windowsill always reminds you of a particular cartoon character, and the tropical climber, you proudly note, has doubled in size in the past year.

Many people talk to their plants, and it can be beneficial to both parties. Perhaps when you sing lovingly to your spider plant during the day, you up the level of carbon dioxide, thereby increasing the production of sugar in the leaves through photosynthesis. It might be that your hot breath also raises the humidity around its leaves, something a spider plant adores. But equally, it might not.

However, showing your plant a bit of attention means you'll get to know its needs – you'll notice dust accumulating on its leaves (blocking that all-important light), a limpness that means it's being over- or underwatered, yellowing foliage that indicates the compost is exhausted, or crispy leaves that are a sign it's getting too much light.

And being in tune with the living things around you is good for the soul. You don't need proof of that, surely?

'I used to go with my mum to the garden centre, and the small cacti were near the tills. When I was six or seven, I started growing them – actually, I usually killed them within a month! My tip for plant novices is: don't care for them too much. When you're starting out, you tend to overwater and overfeed them, or set them back by repotting them too often, particularly indoor plants. Take a step back. Neglect them a bit.'

Paul Rees, tender and tropical plant specialist, Kew

Part Two: Plants

The world of plants is mesmerisingly rich and diverse.

Whatever your style and whatever your space, there is a fascinating and beautiful plant that's just right for you.

Go on. Get it. Share it.

Dramatic

———

Your living space is theatrical, a stage where great
stories unfold. Sumptuous textures, intense colours,
a lively interplay of light and shade, music and conversation
make for a stimulating creative environment. You are at
home at the Palm Court tea dance, you revel in the glamour
of the five-star hotel in the old town, you glide across the
black and white floor tiles of a grand conservatory.

These plants have strong personalities. Like A-list actors,
their bold charismatic presence commands attention.
Rooms reconfigure around them. Unlike actors, they are
neither demanding nor tricky to care for. Coming from rich
tropical and subtropical forests, they are accustomed
to competition and are robust and self-reliant.
The only thing they can't stand is frost.

Flamboyant foliage / forest bromeliads / island trees / climbers

Opposite, painted glory: the lush leaves of the peacock plant

Flamboyant foliage from forest floors

Dumb cane / elephant's ear / rattlesnake plant/ peacock plant

Why grow them? For their impressive evergreen foliage, with lots of different textures, patterns, colours and shapes to choose from.

What's the story? They come from tropical forests where light levels are low beneath the dense tree canopy. These plants of the understorey and forest floor have evolved large broad leaves to catch as much light as possible. Humidity is high and heavy rain pelts down through the canopy. Like many broad-leaved plants, they have pointed tips known as 'drip tips', so they can shed rainwater easily. This means algae can't grow on the leaf surface – if they did, they would act as sun block, reducing the plant's ability to photosynthesise.

With their big, beautifully patterned leaves, it's no surprise that rattlesnake (*Calathea lancifolia*) and peacock (*Calathea makoyana*)

plants come from tropical forests in the Americas. Dumb cane (*Dieffenbachia seguine*) and elephant's ear (*Alocasia*) belong to the arum family. Its members include some of the smelliest characters in the plant kingdom. To attract their insect pollinators (usually flies), many produce flowers that emit a gruesome smell, often like rotting flesh. The titan arum produces the biggest unbranched flower spike in the world, up to 3 m (10 ft) tall. When it is ready for pollination, the flower spike heats up to human body temperature, which helps the vile smell waft further through the rainforest. Tellingly, it's also called the corpse flower. You'll be glad to know that most arum houseplants flower very rarely, if ever.

What they like Bright, indirect light, warmth (+15°C/60°F) and humidity.

What they loathe High temperatures and bright light. Sitting in waterlogged compost.

How to grow them Indoors, in a warm bright place that doesn't get direct sun. Plant in free-draining compost in a pot no bigger than their existing root system, repotting only as it gets really congested (see *Potting on* on page 227). Wipe the dust from their leaves now and again with a soft damp cloth. Stand their pots on a

saucer containing a layer of gravel and water, which will evaporate, raising the humidity around their foliage. Even tropical forests have drier and wetter seasons, and house plants from these habitats are healthier if they are allowed a period of rest, in the low light of winter, when water and feeding should be reduced.

Look out for Other great plants from the arum family that are grown for their flowers – the peace lily (*Spathiphyllum*, see picture on page 201) and flamingo flower (*Anthurium*) – and they smell just fine.

Rex begonias (*Begonia rex*) with origins in the mountain forests of northern India, make wonderful foliage plants for smaller indoor spaces.

And for outside Fatsia (*Fatsia japonica*) is a large glossy-leaved evergreen shrub, while the big, textured leaves of plantain lilies (*Hosta*) unfurl in spring and die down each winter. From the temperate forests of the Far East, these plants are hardy in all but the coldest regions.

Far left, deep purple veining on an alocasia's huge leaves; left, the striking bracts of the flamingo flower; above, the variegation of the dumb cane looks as though a pot of paint has been thrown at it; above right, the undulating margins of quilted *Hosta* leaves provide similar rich textures out of doors.

Forest bromeliads

Urn plant / tufted air plant / flaming sword

Why grow them? For their fascinating foliage and brilliant flower bracts.

What's the story? They come from the rainforests of Central and South America and some Caribbean islands. Unlike their relative the pineapple, which is a ground dweller, these are primarily epiphytes, growing in the trees or on rocks, clinging with roots that never reach the soil. They collect rainwater in the deep cup in the centre of their rosettes. Detritus from other plants and animals also falls into the cup and decays, giving them the nutrients they need. They are pollinated by hummingbirds, which feed on the rich nectar of the short-lived flowers. These are produced over a long period from showy, brightly coloured bracts.

What they like Bright, indirect light and humidity.

What they loathe Hot sunshine, dry air and extended cold periods.

How to grow them Indoors, in a warm bright place that doesn't get direct sun. Plant in a loose bark compost in a pot that's no bigger than their existing root system, repotting only as it gets really congested (see *Potting on* on page 227).

SHARE ALERT

It takes around five years before bromeliads start to flower, so mature plants can be expensive. After flowering, the plant will slowly die. But don't panic! Like lots of rosette plants, a mature plant produces 'offsets' known as pups (ahhh). Detach them from the parent and pot them up (though be patient – don't do it too early). Grow them on and give spares to your friends. Enjoy their handsome foliage for between one and three years, until in turn they get big enough to flower.

Look out for Urn plant (*Aechmea fasciata*) – leathery arched leaves, with a silver and sea-green patina, overlap in a rosette creating a ladder of watertight 'urns'. At maturity the plant produces a series of small blue flowers over a long period of time, on vivid pink bracts.

Tufted air plant (*Guzmania lingulata*) – glossy green leaves with smooth margins and brilliant pink or red flower bracts (sometimes even yellow and orange) that can last up to four months (see picture on page 205).

Flaming sword (*Vriesea splendens*) – stiff green leaves with dark irregular bands across them, plus a bright red, flattened, long-lasting spike of yellow flowers that each last only a day. Imagine the excitement when this plant was first brought to Europe in 1840 (see picture on page 197).

'The pot plant I wouldn't be without is *Vriesea splendens*, the first houseplant I ever bought and the one that started me on the journey I'm on today. It always reminds me there is more to learn! I grow it in the bedroom on an east-facing windowsill (morning light with early direct sun) – probably not ideal, as it prefers more humid air (like a kitchen or bathroom), but it is doing well. In the wild, it grows as an epiphyte attached to other plants up in the air and nowhere near the soil. It collects water in the leaves to feed itself and can also be a home to tree frogs.'

Scott Taylor, temperate plants specialist, Kew

Spiky! The flowers, bracts and foliage of the forest bromeliads make you sit up and take notice. Opposite, the brilliant bracts and, above, the foliage of the urn plant. In the wild, near left, they grow high in the branches of other trees – or sometimes on rocks

Island trees

Areca palm / dragon tree / Kentia palm

Why grow them? Complex foliage, air detox (they all feature in NASA's top 50 plants for cleaning indoor air) and stature – they can reach 2 m (7 ft) when container grown, though that's nothing compared to their height in the tropical forests that are their native habitats.

What's the story? They come from the islands of the southern oceans.

Areca palm (*Dypsis lutescens*) has sharply defined, arching yellow-green fronds arising from multiple stems. Container plants can reach more than 2 m (7 ft). This palm comes from the rainforests of Madagascar, where it grows up to 12 m (40 ft), in sandy soil near the sea.

Dragon tree (*Dracaena marginata*) has a head of stiff, spiky-looking, glossy, red-edged green leaves set at the top of a slender, scaly grey trunk or cane. This plant comes from Madagascar, Mauritius and other nearby islands of the Indian Ocean.

Kentia or sentry palm (*Howea forsteriana*), the most popular decorative palm in the world, comes from the tiny volcanic Lord Howe Island in the Tasman Sea. It has lovely erect stems with arching fronds of long slender leaflets and can grow to 3 m (10 ft) tall in pots (gulp). It copes very well in the dry atmosphere that comes with central heating – almost all other palms turn brown at the leaf tips, but the Kentia maintains its intense dark-green integrity. It is also very happy in a shady room.

What they like Bright indirect light and warmth (+15°C/60°F).

What they loathe Hot sunshine, extended cold periods and soggy compost.

How to grow them Indoors, in a warm bright place out of direct sun, in a standard indoor compost mix. Let the surface of the compost dry out between waterings. They thrive at room temperature and suffer in the cold. If you repot them every other year into fresh compost, they don't need additional feeding. Wipe dust from the leaves now and again with a soft damp cloth (a lovely meditative practice).

Also look out for Umbrella tree (*Schefflera actinophylla*) from the tropical rainforests of Australia, whose fruit is eaten by flying foxes. Parlour palm (*Chamaedorea elegans*) the must-have plant of the 19th-century drawing room – from the wet forests of Central America. Ponytail palm or elephant's foot (*Beaucarnea recurvata*) – whose swollen trunk is adapted for water storage in the drought conditions of its arid Mexican habitat. Bottle palm (*Hyophorbe lagenicaulis*) from the island of Mauritius.

'Palm trees got me into plants. I'd grown up in London and I'd never seen anything like them. I love the sun and they remind me of tropical places.'

John Bloomfield, seasonal displays specialist, Kew

Far left, dragon tree and areca palm come from tropical islands of the Indian ocean; left, Kentia palms growing on Lord Howe Island (photo: William J Baker, RBG Kew); above left, the parlour palm and right, the umbrella tree.

Social climbers

Heart-leaf plant / devil's ivy

Why grow them? Fascinating trailing and climbing foliage that makes them versatile subjects for lots of bright to shady indoor spaces.

What's the story? In forests, competition for light and food is fierce. Instead of putting all their energies into building their own woody structures to gain height, climbers are opportunists, clambering up other plants to head towards the light. Think of ivy (*Hedera*), which climbs using rootlets to cling, and honeysuckle (*Lonicera*), which twines itself around the limbs of its neighbours to get ahead in the search for the sun.

The race to the light is even more extreme in the tropics and subtropics, and there is a wealth of plants that have adapted to climb. Some of them make great houseplants. Domesticating them tends to slow them down a bit, which is no bad thing as in their native habitats they can reach dimensions that would soon outgrow the average apartment!

Heart-leaf plant (*Philodendron scandens*) – has glossy green leaves that are – wait for it – heart shaped, on twining stems that can reach 3m (10ft) tall. From humid tropical forests of Central America, it climbs with the aid of aerial roots. As does devil's ivy (*Epipremnum aureum*, often labelled as *Scindapsus aureus*). This one's a whopper in its natural environment, climbing 20 m (65 ft) up the slender trees of the tropical forests of South Pacific islands in its search for light. In the house it reaches a less daunting 2 m (6 ft).

What they like Bright to shady conditions with moderate to high humidity.

What they loathe Direct sunshine, draughts and waterlogged soil.

How to grow them Indoors, in a warm bright to shady place that doesn't get direct sun (they will grow less vigorously in lower light levels). Use a standard houseplant compost mix and allow the surface to dry between waterings. Add liquid feed fortnightly during the growing season and reduce to monthly feeding in winter. Train to a frame or allow to tumble from a hanging basket or shelf (see *Macramé central* on page 171).

Also look out for Climbers with summer flowers, including the wax plant (*Hoya carnosa*) from eastern Asia and Australia, and bridal wreath (*Stephanotis floribunda*) from Madagascar. Both need a bright place out of direct sunlight, produce waxy fragrant flowers in summer and can grow to 4 m (12 ft) indoors.

For winter flowers, try star jasmine (*Jasminum polyanthum*), a woody vine from subtropical open forests in the mountains of China and Burma. It's a vigorous plant, growing to 10 m (33 ft) in the wild and is an invasive weed in some parts of the world, so keep it indoors in the sunshine and under control! You'll be rewarded, in winter, by fragrant white starry flowers.

Far left, rainforest climbers, including a species of heart-leaf plant (photo: Rebecca Hilgenhof); above left, next to a mass of spiderettes from a spider plant, devil's ivy tumbles from a shelf; top right, heart-leaf plant trained over a circular structure; bottom right, the fragrant flowers of star jasmine appear in winter.

Edible

Are your taste buds discerning? And do you care
about the quality of the fuel you put into your body?
Is it important to you to buy local produce, in season?

No food is as good as the food you have grown yourself,
and it is doubly delicious when freshly picked. From
plot to plate in a few minutes, your crops have lost none
of their nutrients. Your only challenge is to wait until
the food is absolutely ready to harvest. Anticipation
can be beautiful torture.

All of these plants have been domesticated by ingenious
gardeners, who have selected, crossed and backcrossed
using all manner of clever genetic manipulation
to produce delectable food to meet the whimsical
ever-changing taste of the public.

Lettuces / chilli peppers and tomatoes / strawberries

Salad days

Lettuce

Why grow them? Fresh and frilly, ornamental, colourful. The humble lettuce (*Lactuca*) has been coaxed by generations of vegetable gardeners into a wealth of varieties. There are sweet, compact 'Little Gem', refreshing butterheads, red frills with health-giving bitter compounds, and peppery leaves that tingle your taste buds.

What's the story? The wild lettuce is an annual plant called *Lactuca sativa*, which is actually in the daisy family. It was domesticated by the ancient Egyptians. Over the centuries many different varieties have been developed and they are eaten all over the world, valued as a source of vitamins K (blood clotting, strong bones) and A (growth, disease resistance and vision).

What they like Sunshine, fresh air and free-draining compost.

What they loathe Very high temperatures, drought and slugs.

How to grow them Outdoors in a bright spot, ideally with shade from the midday sun. Lettuce is one of the best vegetables for growing in containers. Many garden centres and farmers' markets sell small plants grown in little blocks of soil (called plugs) that you simply plant into a container. Lettuces are also extremely easy to grow from seed (see *Sowing seeds* on page 232). The trick is to thin them out (eat the thinnings as a garnish), to give the others plenty of space to grow.

How to harvest Many lettuce varieties can be harvested over a long period – snip a few leaves and more will sprout (known as 'cut-and-come-again'). Or you can harvest the entire head of more compact varieties such as 'Little Gem'.

Surprises Although we associate lettuces with summer salads, they are adapted to cool climates. A prolonged hot, dry spell will put the plants under stress, prompting them to 'bolt' – this is them doing what comes naturally, producing flowers and then seeds to ensure the next generation. But when a lettuce bolts, it's curtains for your salads, as the leaves become bitter and less tasty. Prevent bolting by keeping your plants well watered and shade them when things hot up.

Look out for Loose-leaf (or non-hearting) varieties – 'Lollo Rossa', 'Lollo Verde', oak-leaf, and batavia.
'Little Gem' and other Cos-type varieties.
Other easy salad leaves – including rocket, spinach and nasturtiums.
Leaves for winter – mizuna and lamb's lettuce.

PS Apparently lettuce has sedative properties, so plan a siesta after your delicious leafy lunch.

The best vegetable for container growing, lettuce has been developed into many different cultivars, making it ornamental as well as delicious

Edibles of the nightshade family

Chilli peppers / tomatoes

Why grow them? As good looking as they are tasty, both chilli peppers and tomatoes make eye-catching plants in pots and windowboxes. After harvesting their wonderful fruits, you can compost the plants. Or, if your plant has given you a tasty crop that you'd like to repeat, leave a couple of fruits on the plant until they shrivel up, then save the seeds to sow the following year.

What's the story? Chilli peppers (*Capsicum annuum*) and tomatoes (*Solanum lycopersicum*) come from Central and South America. Chilli peppers have been cultivated for more than 6,000 years in Mexico, tomatoes for at least 2,500 years. Once 15th-century European explorers discovered their delights, they spread around the world like wildfire. We think of chillies as an integral part of South Asian cooking, but they weren't imported to India until the end of the 15th century. Likewise, the tomato is a key ingredient of Italian cuisine but wasn't adopted as food until the 17th century. Until then, it was thought to be poisonous (like the similar-looking European plant, deadly nightshade) and was prized as a purely ornamental plant.

Peppers are categorised by their fruits: bell peppers, sweet peppers, and hot – or chilli - peppers. Chilli peppers are then subdivided according to their heat. Tomatoes are divided by their growth habit – upright (cordon), bush and tumbling (tumbling varieties are great for a deep hanging basket).

What they like Sunshine, rich soil and regular watering.

What they loathe Shade, and sitting in water.

How to grow them Outdoors in large pots, windowboxes or growbags after all danger of frost is past (you can grow the chillies indoors if you have no outside space).

Tomatoes and chilli peppers have the same growing requirements. Grow them from seed (see *Sowing seeds* on page 232) or buy young plants starting them off indoors.

Stake chillies with a stick for support and pinch out the main shoot tip when plants get to 30 cm (1 ft) tall to encourage branching. The first flowers should appear while they're still indoors.

When there's no further danger of frosts, plant your young tomato plants outside in their final position, where there is lots of room for their roots to spread. Stake upright tomatoes, creating a single stem plant by pinching out the shoots that start to grow in the leaf joints. Once your plant has produced four sets of flower trusses, pinch out the growing tips. Allow bush and tumbling tomatoes to shoot all over the place for a heavy, juicy crop. Water them thoroughly and regularly, adding a liquid tomato feed to the water (for chillies too!) every fortnight.

Chilli peppers and tomatoes self-pollinate. They have 'perfect' flowers – with the male and female parts on the same blossom – and depend on the wind to shake the flowers so the anthers release the pollen onto the stigma. But in a sheltered location, to ensure complete fertilisation, gently tap your plant branches every day. (In commercial tomato farms, where the crops are raised under cover, bumblebee colonies are actively encouraged. As the bumblebees visit the flowers they vibrate, causing the anthers to release the pollen – so-called 'buzz pollination'.)

How to harvest Chilli peppers: harvest the fruits regularly to encourage the plant to produce more. For the best colour and flavour – either for eating fresh or drying – allow some to ripen. The brighter red they become, the hotter they usually taste!

Tomatoes: pick them when they are ripe – they should be fully coloured and come away from the plant easily when you pluck them – perfect, juicy explosions of sweet flavour.

Good looking and tasty too:
tomatoes and chilli peppers

Summer pudding

Strawberry

Why grow them? Who doesn't love a strawberry? This plump fragrant flavour-ball sings of summer puddings and picnics. Even though they come into their own in summer, the robust, evergreen plants are handsome enough to grow among your flowers. They themselves produce pretty white flowers, followed by pale fruits with yellow seeds dotted over the surface. As the fruits swell and ripen, their colour and aroma builds in intensity.

What's the story? The wild strawberry (*Fragaria vesca*) grows in forests and fields throughout the northern hemisphere. The Romans used it medicinally, but it wasn't brought into European gardens until the Middle Ages, when it also began to appear in European art. But we have the Americas to thank for the strawberry that is now produced commercially to the tune of more than four million tons per year. *Fragaria × ananassa* is a cross between two species – *Fragaria virginiana* from eastern North America and *Fragaria chiloensis* from Chile – that was made in France in the mid-18th century.

What they like Full sun or partial shade. Good air movement. Sandy soil.

What they loathe Drought during fruit formation.

How to grow them Outdoors in pots, windowboxes, deep hanging baskets or even a length of guttering set at a very slight gradient, to ensure water drains out. Growing in containers means it's easier to protect them from slugs and snails, who will make a soggy mash of the fruits given half a chance.

Using multi-purpose compost, plant your strawberries 25 cm (10 in) apart with the crown (where the leaves emerge) sitting on the surface. Keep them well watered and once the flowers have emerged, add liquid tomato feed to your watering can every two weeks, to help fruit production. After fruiting, remove all the old foliage, just leaving some near the centre of the plant.

How to harvest Once the fruit is a uniform red colour, pick it, together with its little toupée of green leaves.

SHARE ALERT

Strawberries put out stems called runners, which root where they touch the ground, forming a new plant. The runner connecting the mother plant to the new plant eventually shrivels and dies, leaving a new independent strawberry plant. When your strawberry plant produces runners, pin a couple of them down to make sure they touch the surface of the compost, wait for the new plants to root, then detach and share. (And of course, if you know anyone who grows strawberries, ask them for a few rooted runners to get your strawberry growing started too.)

'In our flat we had a little pot of alpine strawberries on the windowsill. They're low maintenance and evergreen and flower all year. When we moved and got a garden, we took them with us and they're now romping away in a flowerbed.'

Suzie Jewell, gardens designer, Kew

Elegant

———

Curves, not angles. Co-ordination, not clash.
Fresh, not fusty. Your living space is light, balanced,
clutter-free. It's not that you're a minimalist, but you
do like your surroundings to be controlled and classy.
Whether the objects on your shelves come from
a flea market or an up-market emporium, they are
sleek and elegant.

The plants on these pages are classics – refined and
beautiful. The daffodils and tulips and moth orchids
carry their precisely defined flowers on erect slender
stems. Complex fronds unfurl from the croziers of the
ferns. Bowls of delicate fragrance open from exquisite
rosebuds. Plants for the connoisseur.

Bulbs / ferns / moth orchids / roses

Opposite, delicate arching fronds of maidenhair fern

Bulbs

Daffodils / tulips / hyacinths / lilies / hippeastrums

Why grow them? Bulbs are all about the seasons. Bursts of colour that light up spring, sensational displays in summer, fresh perfection among the decay of early autumn. Bulbous plants are treasured for their showy flowers, held aloft on slender stems.

What's the story? A bulb is the technical term for the swollen part of the plant where food is stored. It enables the plant to disappear underground at some point in the year to avoid drought, cold or other adverse conditions. Being able to store food and water while you take a break until the weather comes good gives you a competitive advantage in that harsh world out there.

Daffodils were grown in gardens by the ancient Greeks, tulips and hyacinths by tenth-century Persians. Lilies were symbols of hope for the Romans. The Europeans – always eager to turn a profit – stoked a raging speculative market for tulips as status symbols in the 17th century. Amazingly, the most highly prized tulips were those whose flowers were distorted by a virus.

Where they come from Many bulbs have evolved in climates with extreme seasons – perhaps hot and dry like the open steppe of western Asia, where tulips come from, or dry shade, like the northern hemisphere forests where many lilies originate. Daffodils come from the forests and mountains of Europe and North Africa, with the greatest number of species in Spain and Portugal. Daffodils, hyacinths, tulips and lilies are pollinated by insects. Hippeastrums (also known as amaryllis), with their magnificent trumpet-shaped flowers, come from the forests of Central and South America and are pollinated by hummingbirds.

How to grow them Daffodils, tulips and hyacinths: outdoors in pots of free-draining compost in the sunshine. Plant the bulbs in autumn, to a depth of two and a half times their height. They need a period of cold to flower well, so overwinter their containers outside. Once the shoots start to push up through the soil, water regularly.

Lilies: outdoors in soil-based multipurpose compost. Plant the bulbs in autumn to a depth of two and a half times their height. They need a period of cold to flower well the following season, so overwinter them outside. Once the shoots appear, water regularly.

Hippeastrums: indoors (they are frost tender) in a free-draining compost on a bright warm windowsill. Plant so that two-thirds of the bulb is exposed to the air, water well and leave. When the tips of the flower stem and leaves appear (every time it's like a miracle), start watering regularly. The plants usually bloom during winter or spring, six to ten weeks after the bulb is planted.

For all these bulbs, once the flowers have gone over, cut off the flower stems, but allow the leaves to keep on growing until they too

begin to die down. Flowering takes a lot out of a bulb, and the leaves have to work hard to replenish its stores for the following year. Help it out by giving the plant a regular liquid feed until the leaves begin to die down (see *Feeding* on page 226). Once the leaves have faded, knock the soil off the bulbs, dry them out and store them until it's time to plant them again. Or leave them in their pots in a sheltered place where they won't get waterlogged. Inside, you can stop watering them for about eight to ten weeks (their dormant period), until they start into action again.

For late winter indoors: hippeastrums/amaryllis (*Hippeastrum,* see picture on page 201). For spring sunshine outdoors: tulips (*Tulipa*), daffodils (*Narcissus*), hyacinths (*Hyacinthus*). For early summer, in full sun outdoors: ornamental onions (*Allium*). For high summer, in part-shade outdoors: lilies (*Lilium*), Dutch irises (*Iris × hollandica*).

Left, daffodils growing wild in a mountain meadow, north-west Germany (photo: Andreas Groeger); above left, the flouncy hyacinth is also super-fragrant; above right, tulips make fantastic pot-plants. Overleaf, daffodils catch the spring sunshine

Primitive beauty

—

Ferns

Why grow them? Otherworldly, curious and green, this group of plants brings textures and interesting shapes and shadows to indoor and outdoor spaces. Ferns became super fashionable in mid-19th century Europe and unscrupulous collectors rampaged through the countryside driving many species to extinction. The craze for ferns – known as pteridomania – may have subsided, but still these plants add a distinctive elegance to indoor and outdoor spaces.

What's the story? Ferns have been around for a long time, first appearing in the fossil record 360 million years ago, way before the dinosaurs. Flowering plants evolved even later. Ferns growing 300 million years ago helped to form the coal seams that humans have been exploiting in the past few hundred years, contributing to the climate change we are now experiencing. Don't blame the ferns though!

Ferns have stems, leaves and roots, but they don't produce flowers or seeds, instead shedding spores, which then produce tiny plants. Their leaves are structured as fronds, which usually unfurl from beautiful spiral fiddleheads or croziers. The fiddleheads of some species are considered a culinary delicacy, for example, bracken fiddleheads are popular in Japan (despite studies suggesting they are carcinogenic!).

The fronds can be simple and entire, like the hart's tongue fern (*Asplenium scolopendrium*) pictured left, or divided, like the maidenhair fern (*Adiantum raddianum* 'Fragrans') pictured on page 44. Many ferns are epiphytes, growing not in the soil but raised up on rocks or on trees.

Left, Hart's tongue fern; opposite bottom, Boston fern; opposite top, ferns growing on the branch of a tree in Cornwall, south-west England; far right, the classic 'fiddlehead' of a young frond unfurling

Where they come from While there are some dryland species, most ferns come from damp, sheltered, shady habitats. They can be miniscule, like the filmy ferns that are only a few cells thick, or large and robust, like the tree ferns of the southern hemisphere. Ferns have been evolving for aeons and although they are primitive compared to flowering plants, they hold their own, particularly in the moist tropics and subtropics.

What they like Shade to bright indirect light, free-draining compost and humidity.

What they loathe Direct sunlight, temperature swings and dry air.

Look out for
Outdoors:
Male fern (*Dryopteris filix-mas*)
Painted fern (*Athyrium niponicum*)
Hart's tongue fern (*Asplenium scolopendrium*)
Western sword fern (*Polystichum munitum*)

Indoors:
Maidenhair fern (*Adiantum raddianum* 'Fragrans')
Boston fern (*Nephrolepis exaltata* 'Bostoniensis')
Blue Star fern (*Phlebodium aureum*)

Always make sure that the ferns you buy have been produced in cultivation, not collected from the wild (see *Provenance* on page 219).

Surprises Instead of flowers and seeds, ferns produce tiny spores that waft about on the air. If they eventually land in a place with enough moisture, they germinate into a tiny delicate plant called a prothallus. This produces male and female cells that fuse to create a new adult fern. Many ferns are easily grown from spores. If you'd like to give it a try, you could join a fern society with an active spore exchange programme and grow your own. Woah.

Higher plants

Moth orchid

Why grow them? Orchids arouse passion. Their good looks, coupled with their unusual growth habits and their fascinating relationships with other plants, animals and fungi have driven obsessed collectors wild for centuries.

Moth orchids (*Phalaenopsis*) were the first tropical orchids to be grown widely in the 19th century and they are simply fantastic houseplants – undemanding, happy in shade, producing spikes of showy waxy flowers above their rounded fleshy leaves. The display can go on for months, at any time of year.

What's the story? They originate in tropical Asia, from India to Java and the Philippines, and one species even comes from northern Australia. They are epiphytes, growing on trees rather than in the soil, using their snake-like grey roots to cling (without harming the tree). Each species has co-evolved with its pollinating insect: for example the Indonesian moth orchid *Phalaenopsis amabilis* is pollinated by carpenter bees. In fact, most orchids depend on a single species of bird, bee or other insect for pollination, so if that creature dies out, the orchid that depends on it will become threatened with extinction.

What they like Moth orchids are happy in the temperatures we're happy in! But they like a bit more humidity, especially in winter when central heating makes our well-sealed homes dry. Give their leaves a spray with rainwater now and again (take them outside in summer downpours – having a plant in your arms transforms the experience, honest). As they're not soil dwellers, the compost you pot them up in is there only to provide stability and to maintain humidity around the roots.

What they loathe Sitting in water for any length of time.

Opposite, moth orchid with devil's ivy on a bright shelf; right, a moth orchid clings to a forest tree in Laos (photo: Andre Schuiteman)

How to grow them You can buy orchid compost or make it yourself using a mix of three parts washed bark chips and one part shredded leaves or chopped sphagnum moss. Orchids are usually sold in transparent plastic pots, because they enjoy some light on their roots. If you do want to put them in a nice container, make sure it's spacious, so that light can reach in. Grow them in a bright spot which doesn't get direct sunlight. Water and mist plants regularly with rainwater.

When you've become a moth orchid ninja, you can progress further into the extraordinary treasure trove of the family Orchidaceae – one of the largest plant families in the world. There are thousands of different types, and breeders have found ways to hybridise them so that the diversity of flower colour, shape, scent and size boggles the mind. Growing orchids from seed is a technically difficult process – they produce huge quantities of tiny dust-like seeds (up to three million in a seed capsule) that have no food store (in contrast to most other seeds), so in order to germinate they need to grow alongside a specific fungus that supplies them with nutrients. It can take up to ten years for an orchid to grow from seed to flower. So how is it possible to trade orchids at such reasonable prices? In the past few decades, scientists have mastered micro-propagation, whereby clones of parent plants are produced using just a few cells grown in the laboratory.

Floral classic

—

Rose / bougainvillea / hibiscus

Why grow them? Colour, flowers, fragrance and growth habit. People have always been entranced and intrigued by roses. There is evidence they were cultivated in China 5,000 years ago and throughout the Middle East during Roman times. They are a contemporary symbol of love and beauty, but they have also played their part in politics, with white and red roses representing the two rival factions in England's 15th-century Wars of the Roses for example.

Rose species grow naturally throughout the northern hemisphere, as ground cover, shrubs and climbers, in arid regions, steppe, mountains and forests. Their simple flowers are followed by 'hips' – orange, red or purple fruits, the classic colours that attract birds, which feed on them in autumn and winter, dispersing the seeds.

Thousands of years in cultivation means that whatever your outdoor space you can bet there's a rose for it. Many rose cultivars can be grown in containers – patio or miniature roses have been developed for that very purpose – and there are well-behaved climbers and shrubs for sun and shade (some have even had their defensive thorns bred out of them).

What they like Space: roses have long roots, so your container needs to be at least 30 cm (1 ft) deep.

Food: they are hungry plants and need a rich, well-drained soil-based compost and a fortnightly feed through the summer. Repot them every two years, pruning their strongest roots to encourage the production of a fibrous root system.

Air: give them good air circulation and prune them regularly (see *Pruning and deadheading* on page 230).

What they loathe Waterlogged soil or dry soil (which is the main cause of powdery mildew).

Also look out for other elegant floral shrubs with a tropical vibe:

Bougainvillea (*Bougainvillea × buttiana*) – this evergreen climber has conquered the world, thanks to its exuberant displays. Its tiny white flowers are surrounded by brilliantly coloured, papery bracts (modified leaves) that light up in the sun. And brilliant sun is what bougainvilleas need as they come from the open, rocky hillsides of South America. Summer outdoors, winter indoors, unless you live in a frost-free area.

The Chinese rose (*Hibiscus rosa-sinensis*), the national flower of Malaysia, likes a warm bright or sunny spot indoors, without too much fluctuation in temperature. An evergreen shrub with glossy green leaves, it bears brilliant red funnel-shaped flowers and can grow to 1 m (3 ft). Hibiscus fans have developed many cultivars with single and double flowers in colours that range from white through yellow and orange to scarlet and shades of pink. It appreciates a summer holiday outside in the garden or on the balcony.

Left, the ingenuity of plant breeders has produced the complex ruffles of English rose 'Anne Boleyn' and, far right, a range of colours for the naturally red hibiscus; above, the sumptuous colour of the bougainvillea comes from modified leaves surrounding its tiny white flowers

Trashy

———

Loud, proud and positive, you surround yourself
with colour. The more vibrant and clashing the better.
Your place is Googie style, pop art writ large or
space-age synthetics. Bright plastics, techno-fabrics
in vibrant cartoon colours. Your place is fun.

These trashy tender-hearted plants love spending
the summer outdoors. Eye-catching and long-flowering,
with crazy colours and lush foliage. They are the product
of the ingenuity and persistence of amateur and
professional gardeners, who have taken their natural
character and played with it.

These plants have spawned dedicated societies, whose
members generously share their knowledge and their
plants. Do a search online. You might be lucky enough
to have a society near you. It's a true pleasure to meet
someone who really knows their onions, so go to
your local flower show and get chatting.

Pelargoniums / dahlias / petunias / cockscombs

Outrageous! Some cockscomb cultivars, pictured left, push the bounds of good taste

Long-lasting lovelies

Pelargonium

What's the story? Garden pelargoniums have their origins in dry rocky places in south-western South Africa, which, like the Mediterranean, gets most of its rainfall in winter and has warm dry summers. No wonder they do so well so far from home. Some have highly scented foliage to ward off grazing animals in their natural habitat. Pelargonium oil (usually sold as geranium oil) is used widely in aromatherapy as a relaxant.

What they like A warm sunny or partially shaded, sheltered location in summer.

What they loathe Frost and overwatering.

How to grow them Outside in summer. Grow in multi-purpose compost with added grit or sand to ensure good drainage. Water thoroughly, but allow the compost to dry out between waterings – they produce more flowers if kept on the dry side. Deadhead regularly to keep them flowering.

Pelargoniums are often grown as annuals, but you can overwinter them indoors if you have room. Before the first autumn frosts, cut them back to half their size and bring the pots inside to a bright, cool but frost-free windowsill. Keep them fairly dry throughout the winter. When they start to regrow in spring, resume watering. In mid-spring, repot overwintered plants or cuttings into a multi-purpose compost with added grit, pinching out the shoot tips to encourage bushy growth. Place them outside once all risk of frost has passed and they will repay your care with another fantastic display all summer long.

Look out for Ivy-leaved pelargoniums – with their trailing stems, they work well in hanging baskets.

Why grow them? Nothing speaks of whitewashed sun-drenched Greek island villages like brilliant pelargoniums (sometimes incorrectly called geraniums), adorning windowboxes and hanging baskets and spilling from pots on doorsteps in the narrow cobbled streets.

The many species offer amazing diversity, and plant breeders are continually hybridising them to produce even more. There are different leaf shapes and colours, scented foliage, and trailing, scrambling or compact habits. The flowers range from a single rich shade to petals with delicate veining, dip-died effects, contrasting margins and splashes, in single and double flowers. Pelargoniums look good massed in terracotta pots and in windowboxes. And they flower for six months or more if you look after them well.

SHARE ALERT

You can keep your pellies going over winter by taking cuttings. In fact they are the easiest plants for beginners. Take a few extra to share with friends. See *Taking cuttings* on page 234.

Upright angel and regal pelargoniums – rich flowerheads of stunning colour combinations make them great for pots and windowboxes.

Scented-leaf pelargoniums – often grown indoors, where you can enjoy the lovely fragrances of their leaves. They need an airy sunny windowsill and the same watering regime as their cousins outside.

'I saw wild pelargoniums basking in the hot sunshine on the slopes of Table Mountain in Cape Town, South Africa. There are many species native to southern Africa and these wild plants have been used to make the colourful hybrids we grow in our gardens.'

Richard Wilford, gardens designer, Kew

Opposite, pelargoniums growing wild on a rocky cliff in South Africa (photo: Richard Wilford); coming from free-draining, shallow soils, pelargoniums are classic plants for window boxes and pots; previous page, cascades of tuberous begonia and pelargonium cultivars outside an English pub.

Late summer sunshine

—

Dahlia

Why grow them? The dazzling dahlia. The dippiest, daftest daisy. Larger than life, these flamboyant blooms outshine everything else, showing off from midsummer to the first frosts. After a long period in the limelight in the 19th century, they brought pizazz to dreary suburban gardens of the 1960s and 1970s. But in recent years they fell out of fashion, considered too outrageous and gaudy. What cobblers!

The good news is that they're hip again. Yay! And even better, they're easy to grow in containers and you can bring the best blooms indoors to enjoy as long-lasting cut flowers too.

What's the story? Dahlias come from Mexico, land of intense colours and flavours. Imagine the excitement of the European explorers who came across them in the 16th century. They first imported them to Spain as a food crop, following the Aztec tradition of cultivating

them for their tubers, which are similar to the sweet potato. But they didn't catch on as vegetables. Instead, gardeners set to work creating ever more amazing flower forms – spiky, star-shaped, waterlily-like and pompoms.

What they like Full sun, lots of water in the growing season running through free-draining soil.

What they loathe Frost and sitting in water.

How to grow them Outside in summer in pots of rich compost with good drainage. If you buy them as tubers, plant them in a 30 cm (12 in) diameter pot, at a depth of 10–15 cm (4–6 in), laying the tubers flat. To get them flowering earlier in the season, start them off indoors. Once the tips of the leaves emerge from the soil, start watering. Add liquid feed to their water every two weeks – these plants are hungry as well as thirsty!

Overwintering: the first frost will blacken the leaves, telling you it's time to bring your dahlias indoors. On a dry day, tip out the contents of the pot and knock the soil off the tubers. Cut the flowering stems down to 10 cm (4 in) in length and let the surface moisture evaporate. Keep them in a dry, cool spot at 2–3°C (35–37°F) over winter, covered with a layer of dry compost and wrapped in newspaper to stop them shrivelling up. DON'T FORGET THEM. In spring, they will start to sprout, so simply pot them up in fresh compost. Once the leaves emerge from the compost, resume the summer watering regime and prepare for another show-stopping year.

PS Single or semi-double flowered varieties are best for attracting pollinators. Double flowers are often bred without pollen-producing parts, or have so many petals that it's difficult for bees to find the bounty. So if insects really aren't your thing, look for double flowers.

'I always have *Dahlia* 'Miss Alison' growing, because it was named after me! It's a hybrid of two other dahlia cultivars – red-flowered 'Bishop of Llandaff' and apricot-yellow 'Moonfire' – and it takes its character from both of them. The bees must have cross-pollinated the flowers and I found it growing among a group of 'Moonfire' plants. The flowers start out dark maroon, open to burgundy-red and age to pink.'

Alison Smith, perennials specialist, Kew

Dahlias inspire deep devotion and over the centuries gardeners have created flowers of wonderful complexity and colour

Romper room

Petunia

Why grow them? Think of a traditional English pub in summer and the petunia will come to mind. Great mounds of trailing foliage, funnel-shaped flowers from spring through to the first frost. And what a range of colours! Every hue except true blue, from rich black velvet to crazy pinwheels of pink and yellow, to delicate salmon with a darker veining.

Petunias are great for hanging baskets and windowboxes, and for planting under bigger plants in larger containers. Boggle your mind by planting them alongside clashing tuberous begonias and busy Lizzies. Stealing a few stems for a vase indoors won't cause any sulks – these little troopers will just produce more flowers in response.

What's the story? Petunias come from South America, and are relatives of potatoes, tomatoes, chilli peppers, deadly nightshade and tobacco (imagine that family reunion!). Like many family members, petunias are sticky to the touch and this deters pests such as aphids, who don't fancy getting stuck. Almost all garden petunia cultivars are hybrids of two species – *Petunia axillaris*, whose white flowers open at night and are pollinated by moths, and *Petunia integrifolia*, whose dark purple flowers open in the day and are pollinated by bees. Once the Europeans mastered glasshouse growing in the 19th century, these vibrant plants became a key part of the summer bedding schemes that were all the rage in public parks and posh suburban houses in the 19th century.

What they like Sunshine (although they'll tolerate a few hours of shade) and free-draining compost.

What they loathe Frost and waterlogged soil.

How to grow them Outside in summer. After all risk of frost has passed, plant them out in containers filled with multi-purpose compost.

Water regularly, especially if they're in hanging baskets, which dry out quickly in sun or wind. Deadhead regularly too, nipping off the old flowers to prevent disease and to keep new blooms coming. To maintain flowering until the first frosts, add liquid feed to their water every two weeks from midsummer.

Overwintering: petunias are often treated as annuals and discarded once summer is over, but you can overwinter your favourites indoors, to continue the display the following summer. Before the first autumn frosts, cut them back to 10–15 cm (4–6 in) and bring the pots inside to a bright, cool but frost-free windowsill (or pot them up in smaller pots, to save space). Keep the compost just moist enough to prevent it drying out completely. Pick out and discard fallen leaves to prevent bacterial and fungal diseases. When the plants start to sprout in spring, return to the summer watering regime.

SHARE ALERT

Keep your petunias going over winter by taking cuttings. They root readily, so are ideal for novices. Take a few extra to share with your friends. See *Taking cuttings* on page 234.

Astounding colour all summer long – petunias keep on giving, even in partial shade

Clash of symbols

Cockscomb / tuberous begonia

Why grow them? Big splashes of crazy colour from the flowerheads of the cockscomb (*Celosia*) will outrage the good taste brigade throughout the summer months.

What's the story? Coming from the equatorial tropics around the world, in cooler climes they are grown as annuals and their brilliant blooms – either the weird crest formations or flame-like plumes – come in brash oranges, reds, pinks, yellows and purples. Who would have guessed that such a show-off would also be a valuable leafy green vegetable, similar to spinach? One variety of *Celosia argentea* is the most popular green veg in Nigeria.

What they like Sun, sun, sun and well-drained soil.

'People can be reluctant to use bright-coloured plants and flowers in their gardens, fearing that they are unfashionable. I'm not. We use large numbers in our annual summer bedding schemes, which are one of the major highlights for Kew's summer visitors. I often repeat the themes in my own garden using the surplus. Bright and hot colours lift the mood and are what summer is all about.'

Greg Redwood, tender plants specialist, Kew

What they loathe Shade and soggy compost.

How to grow them Outside in summer, or inside all year. They are easy to grow from seed. Once all chance of frost has passed, transplant your seedlings into pots of free-draining soil-based compost and place in full sun in a sheltered place. Give them a liquid feed every fortnight to encourage flowering.

Also look out for Tuberous begonias (*Begonia* × *tuberhybrida*) – marvellous flim-flam developed from Andean species of this widespread tropical and subtropical genus. These begonias, which grow from tubers, were first hybridised as early as 1870 and breeders have been producing spectacular cultivars ever since, with glossy foliage and large single or double, ruffled or frilled, blotched or single-colour blooms that are pendent or compact. Grow them indoors if you get frosts. Alternatively, grow them outdoors as summer bedding, lifting the tubers in the autumn before the first frost and storing them in a cool dry place. Replant the tubers in spring and grow them on indoors until it's warm enough for them to go outside and do their glorious business all over again.

Cockscombs can be truly outrageous, far left, or more restrained, above left; above night, spectacular cultivars of the tuberous begonia have been produced over the past 150 years

Natural

———

Does hot-house drama leave you cold? Would you rather be wandering through a meadow humming with insects, or sitting in a woodland glade listening to the birds? Do you banish synthetics from your living space – a contemplative place of wood and weave?

Natural plants wax and wane with the seasons, in tune with the cycles of the great outdoors. But natural doesn't mean beige. Flowering plants of meadows and woodland clearings and the rocky flower-rich hillsides of the Mediterranean have evolved to attract insect pollinators. The colour, scent and structure of a flower can give you a good idea of the type of insects that pollinate it. What could be better than watching the precision of a bumblebee foraging in your windowbox, with pantaloons full of protein-rich pollen and a belly full of nectar?

The plants in this section are all grown outside.

Aromatic herbs / daisies / grasses

Opposite, a bumblebee visits the complex blue flowers of love-in-the-mist, with an orange poppy in the background

Aromatic herbs

Lavender / lemon balm / marjoram / mint / rosemary / sage / thyme

What's the story? Some of our most important culinary herbs are members of the mint family. These plants are famous for their wonderful aromas. We're still not sure why they produce their volatile oils: maybe to deter biting insects, such as beetles and caterpillars, or grazing goats; maybe to inhibit the growth of seedlings around mature plants, preventing overcrowding and lessening competition for the nutrients and water during long hot summers. These plants are very important for pollinators, producing flowers over a long period to provide pollen and nectar for bees and butterflies.

COOL MINTS

Mints tolerate more shade and need more watering than their cousins. They also need richer compost, with more organic matter. The most versatile mint is peppermint (*Mentha × piperita*). It produces a volatile oil containing menthol, which is used in tea, chewing gum and toothpaste and famously in Middle Eastern cuisine. Peppermint is a naturally occurring hybrid of two mint species – watermint and spearmint. Like many hybrids, it's an exuberant plant (benefitting from a characteristic known as hybrid vigour) that will quickly take over a garden given the right conditions. Planting it in a container – a big pot or windowbox – is a good way to control it. An ideal position would get sun in the morning and shade in the afternoon, but actually peppermint will take shade all day. In mid- to late summer it produces handsome spikes of pretty purple flowers in whorls around its square stems. It dies back over winter and pops up again in spring, just in time to add a cool hit to your salads and drinks.

Why grow them? Their leaves can be used to flavour your cooking and to make delicious drinks, and their aromatic properties have also been used medicinally for thousands of years. The Romans traded lavender flowers as luxury goods and modern science has shown that lavender combats anxiety and aids sleep. They are fantastic plants for bees and butterflies too, so you get triple the benefits: beauty, biodiversity and health.

'I love cooking, so I've always grown herbs in containers close to the back door, particularly mint, which can be a real thug in the open ground. For most plants in containers I use a soil-based compost. As many herbs come from the Mediterranean, they can tolerate a bit of drought. So if you miss watering them for a few days they usually survive!'

Tony Hall, woody plants specialist, Kew

Where they come from Apart from mint itself (see panel), these plants come from sunny rocky slopes with poor soil and hot dry summers.

What they like They need well-drained soil and will tolerate drought, so they happily grow in pots and other containers. They'll forgive you for abandoning them for a week, as long as you give them a thorough watering as a goodbye present.

What they loathe Cold wet soil in the winter.

Look out for Evergreen shrubs: lavender (*Lavandula*), rosemary (*Rosmarinus*) Herbs: marjoram (*Origanum*), lemon balm (*Melissa*), catnip (*Nepeta*), thyme (*Thymus*), sage (*Salvia*).

How to grow them Outside in pots. Choose a pot that's at least 20 cm (8 in) deep, and put a 2.5 cm (1 in) layer of pebbles or broken pots in the base to aid drainage. Then fill with a soil-based compost. Give your plants a thorough weekly watering in spring and summer, but keep them fairly dry as the cold sets in over winter.

If you have no outside space, grow your herbs on a sunny windowsill, next to a window that is often open (see *Herbs to hand* page 194).

Above, lavender growing wild on a rocky Mediterranean hillside (photo: Tony Hall); left, thyme produces dense spikes of many tiny pink flowers; right, handsome herbs - sage and flowering thyme, with the grass-like foliage of chives and mint behind

Meadow abundance

Daisies

Why grow them? Who is not charmed by meadow flowers? The brilliant colours of daisies, cornflowers, poppies and marigolds dancing above the lush green of crops that are yet to ripen. Just reciting their names magically transports you to the summer countryside!

The ox-eye daisy and its close relatives produce their bright and breezy flowers from late spring. These flowers of the field treasure their freedom and don't need pampering, and you can create a meadow-like vibe in even the smallest containers.

What's the story? Most of the larger members of the daisy family are sun lovers, coming from mountain slopes, grasslands and areas of disturbed ground around the world. They have been hybridised to make fabulous garden plants and with a soil-based compost and regular feeding and watering, you can have a daisy display in a container from spring to autumn. Many of these hybrids are tender, but you can take cuttings during the season and keep them going over winter on a bright cool windowsill with very restricted watering.

Late spring to early summer – choose ox-eye daisies (*Leucanthemum vulgare*) from European meadows, and painted daisies (*Tanacetum coccineum*) from the Caucasus.

All summer long – joyful flowers from marguerites (*Argyranthemum frutescens*) from the Canary Islands, yellow chamomile (*Anthemis tinctoria*) from Europe and Western Asia, yellow ox-eye (*Buphthalmum salicifolium*) from central Europe, African daisy (*Osteospermum*) and blue marguerites (*Felicia amelloides*) from South Africa.

Late summer into autumn – the colour keeps coming with chrysanthemums (*Chrysanthemum* × *morifolium*) from China, Shasta daisies (*Leucanthemum* × *superbum*), North American asters (*Symphyotrichum novae-angliae*) and the Eurasian Michaelmas daisies (*Aster* × *frikartii*).

All the cornfield flowers resent competition from trees and grassland, so they take advantage of ground disturbed by humans and livestock – hence their age-old association with farming.

What they like Well-drained soil and lots of sunshine.

What they loathe Shade, and waterlogged soil.

How to grow them They are easily grown from seed (see *Sowing seeds* on page 232). You can also buy them as plugs or small plants and they'll soon fill their containers. Grow them in a free-draining soil-based compost, allowing it to dry out between waterings.

Deadhead regularly to prolong flowering.

Also look out for
Field poppies (*Papaver rhoeas*)
Cornflowers (*Centaurea cyanus*)
Love-in-the-mist (*Nigella damascena*) see page 68.
California poppies (*Eschscholzia californica*)
Pincushion flowers (*Scabiosa* cultivars such as 'Butterfly Blue') see page 8.

Left, asters flower in Autumn; above, African daisies or osteospermums keep flowering all summer if you deadhead them regularly; daisies, dandelions and their relatives are key ingredients of the incredible floral tapestries of mountain meadows (photo: Katherine Price)

Structure and texture

—

Grasses

Why grow them? In recent decades, grasses have been brought into our gardening spaces, imparting understated elegance and cool counterpoint to all the floral flim-flam. They add texture and movement, and often have highly ornamental seedheads – feathery plumes, furry spikelets or sprays of pale capsules – and fantastic autumn colour, persisting right through to late winter.

What's the story? Grasslands cover a fifth of the world's land surface, from the tropics to the far north and south, but there are also grasses adapted to forests and mountains, bogs or beside lakes and streams. This highly evolved plant family includes fantastically important crops such as wheat, rice and maize – crops that turned hunter-gatherers into farmers, laying the foundations for states and nations. Historical vertigo! Grasses are pollinated by the wind. So they don't need to produce showy blooms or fragrance to attract insects or other creatures to help them produce the next generation. However, they do have pollen-producing flowers (as hay-fever sufferers will tell you), hence the fantastic seedheads.

What they like Difficult to define! There are tall grasses from the prairies that thrive in deep fertile soil in full sun, and grasses from wetter places that like dappled shade. Sedges and reeds love sunny pond margins, while pretty feathertops prefer shallow soils in rocky places.

What they loathe See above.

Left, tall grasses dominate an ancient wet meadow in the Austrian Alps (photo: Katherine Price); above, the dainty flower sprays of wood melick light up a shady corner; near right, the strappy foliage of evergreen sedge *Carex morrowii* 'Ice Dance' has handsome striped margins; far right, blue fescue is a spiky contrast to the flowers on the sunny balcony

How to grow them Use a free-draining soil-based compost mixed with composted bark to open it up. Mulch the surface with composted bark or pebbles to stop weeds establishing. Let the compost dry out between thorough waterings during the growing season, to avoid the soil becoming waterlogged. Cut back deciduous grasses close to ground level between late February and the end of March, before new green shoots start to appear. The cut stems can be left on the soil surface as a natural mulch or composted. In spring, give evergreen grasses a good comb through with your fingers to pull out all the dead foliage and old flowerheads.

Look out for
For sun:
Pheasant's tail grass (*Anemanthele lessoniana*)
Blue fescue (*Festuca glauca*)
Feathertop (*Pennisetum villosum*)
Mexican feather grass (*Nassella* or *Stipa tenuissima*)

For shade:
Sedge (*Carex morrowii* 'Ice Dance')
Wood melick (*Melica uniflora*)
Silver grass (*Miscanthus sinensis*)
Japanese forest grass (*Hakonechloa macra*)

Odd

———

Your living space is an eccentric mish-mash of styles. You can't seem to pass a junk shop or a skip without stopping. Not for you the balanced Scandi vibe of the modern apartment. You surround yourself with objects and images that interest you, whether or not they complement each other. Surreal, unbalanced, stimulating, it's a house of curiosities. In every corner there's something to catch the eye and remind you of the rich diversity of life.

The plants in this section are strange and fascinating – the result of living in niches where most plants wouldn't survive. So they have very particular but straightforward requirements. Your reward? A glimpse into their weird worlds – and plant companions that enrich yours.

Carnivores / living stones / air plants

Opposite, the mysterious insect traps of the pitcher plant

Carnivores

Venus flytraps / pitcher plants

Why grow them? Treasure these curiosities of the plant kingdom for their lurid colours and their precise, alien structures. It's just not possible to pass them by without marvelling at their seductive otherworldliness. But in spite of their strangeness, they are easy, undemanding plants for indoors and outdoors.

What's the story? Head in the hot sun, toes in the marsh. Imagine the ancient, peaty flatlands of the coastal plain in the eastern United States, saturated with water, open to the sky, the occasional pine tree throwing shade from the hot summer sun. Venus flytraps and pitcher plants have adapted to thrive in these subtropical marshes. The swamps are poor in nutrients, so the plants get their essential nitrogen and minerals not through their roots but from above – by trapping and digesting insects. Yum.

They have developed tempting structures to lure their prey into their grasp and trapping mechanisms to keep them there. The main prey of the Venus flytrap (*Dionaea muscipula*), despite its common name, are ants, spiders, beetles and grasshoppers. Each leaf consists of two glistening, red, hinged lobes. When an unsuspecting bug crawls over them, touching two trigger hairs in succession, the lobes snap together in an incredible tenth of a second. By struggling to escape, the bug stimulates the tightening of the trap and the production of digestive enzymes by the plant.

The pitcher plant (*Sarracenia*) has a different strategy, attracting insects with nectar. They can't help but investigate the bright patterns inside the pitcher. It has a waxy, flaking lining that the insects can't grip and they fall into an enzyme soup at the base of the death-slide, where they are broken down into digestible form.

What they like Direct sunshine and a good supply of rainwater.

What they loathe Tap water (as it's too alkaline).

How to grow them Carnivorous plants belong to the handful of plants that really need peat (see *For peat's sake* on page 221). Plant them in a mixture of peat and sharp sand. Use rainwater, placing it in a saucer under the pot rather than pouring it over the plant. Pitcher plants can grow in soggy soil with the water in the saucer halfway up the pot, but Venus flytraps prefer damp soil – stand the pot on a layer of gravel with 6 mm (1/4 in) of water to give them the humidity they like.

Venus fly traps cannot survive frost so grow them on a sunny windowsill. Some pitcher plants are hardy enough to grow outside even

in Northern Europe, if they are given a sunny spot sheltered from the wind. All do well on a cool sunny windowsill or in an unheated porch.

Look out for

The Venus flytrap is unique – there is only one species, so there are no hybrids. But how can you improve on perfection?

Pitcher plants, on the other hand, have been hybridised to produce some weird and wonderful cultivars, with flamboyant colouring and veining of the pitchers.

Left, pitcher plants growing by a lake in Sandhills, North Carolina, USA (photo: Katherine Price); top and right, the patterns on the mouths of the pitchers are deadly lures for insects; bottom left, the lobes of the Venus flytrap snap together in a tenth of a second, snaring their prey

Living stones

Lithops

Why grow them? When is a stone not a stone? When it's a lithops. These plants are masters of disguise, adopting the smooth, rounded shape and intricate patterns of pebbles. Quirky indeed. They grow as a pair of swollen leaves with flat tops that are textured with ridges, warts and wrinkles and sometimes have colourful patterns.

What's the story? Lithops come from the plains of southern Africa (notably the region gloriously known as the Succulent Karoo), which have low rainfall and a long dry season. They have evolved to store water and are relatively fleshy, so would be like sweet little juice-bombs for the herds of grazing animals that roam across these lands. Not so

'The first plants that caught my attention were mesembryanthemums, growing as bedding at the little house in Swansea where we used to spend summer holidays. I must have been about seven or eight. I was fascinated by how the flowers opened and closed over the course of the day.'

Nick Johnson, tender and tropical plants specialist, Kew

great for the lithops, which hug the ground and adopt their stony disguise. Another amazing adaptation of the lithops are their fruit capsules, which are activated by water, meaning they only release seeds at a time when germination is likely to be successful – when it rains! Lithops perform a third great trick during extreme droughts, when they pull themselves down into the soil. This reduces their surface area, minimising water loss.

What they like Strong sunlight and an airy position.

What they loathe Overwatering is the death of lithops. If in doubt, don't. They don't like shade either.

How to grow them They need full sun and very free-draining, poor sandy soil at least 10 cm (4 in) deep, to accommodate their relatively long, fleshy roots. Plants grown in strong light develop tough, strongly coloured skins, but they will struggle in excessive heat. Though they are tolerant of low temperatures, it's best to keep them frost free. Try growing them from seed.

Take a little time to master the watering of lithops. In spring and summer when the plant is dormant, water only if the leaves appear wrinkled. Tap water is fine. As autumn approaches, flowerbuds will appear. At this time water thoroughly every three weeks or so. After the flower dies off, stop watering completely. As the new leaf pair appears in winter, stop watering until the old leaf pair is dry and shrivelled. Then start watering normally again, keeping the compost barely moist.

Surprises In autumn or winter, flowers with many silky slender petals emerge, like little white or yellow miracles from between the leaf pairs. They are often sweetly scented. The flowers open when the sun is shining, from about midday. In their homelands they are pollinated by bees – and possibly moths in the late afternoon.

Also look out for Lithops are in the succulent family Aizoaceae. They are tricky plants to grow, so if you're just starting out, try some of their more laid-back relatives, including icicle plants (*Mesembryanthemum*), *Bergeranthus* and *Delosperma*, for a similar effect. These are widely available from garden centres.

Moonstones (*Pachyphytum oviferum*) is a very special houseleek-relative known from one single location in Mexico on rock cliffs at an altitude of 1,100 m (3,900 ft). Also called the sugared almond plant, its blue-white swollen leaves, sometimes flushed with purple, look like those old-fashioned treats. This 10 cm (3 in) tall oddity produces magnificent red flowers on slender silvery stalks in late winter. Gorgeous and weird, all at once.

Curiouser and curiouser; the mottled, swollen leaf-pairs of the lithops, opposite; above, living stones have evolved to survive the harsh dry lands of Southern Africa

Air plants

—

Tillandsia

Why grow them? With their spiky rigid leaves in muted silvers, greens and pinks, air plants have intriguing textures and structures. As they don't need soil, they can be hung from hooks and shelving. Arrange them with natural objects like shells or driftwood, or adorn your treasured glass or ceramic containers. Hang them outside on your balcony or from your windowsill during summer.

What's the story? Air plants (*Tillandsia*) come from the Americas, in a range of habitats from tropical rainforests to deserts. They are a branch of the bromeliad family (see *Forest bromeliads* on page 28) and like many of their cousins they don't need soil. Instead, they're epiphytic, growing on trees, rocks and cliffs, where they absorb water and nutrients through their leaves. The best-known air plant is Spanish moss (*Tillandsia usneoides*), which hangs in great silver-green sheets from trees in the southern United States and Central America. The air plants we grow as houseplants come from subtropical open woodlands with regular mists or rainfall. A single tree can support thousands of these slow-growing plants.

What they like Bright indirect light, and regular sprays or baths of water.

What they loathe Frost, and sitting in water.

How to grow them Air plants can be placed anywhere. They are not particular about temperature, but are most comfortable between 10°C (50°F) and 30°C (86°F). Just because they don't need soil, doesn't mean they don't need watering. Take your air plant down from its container and spray it thoroughly or rinse it under the tap until it's dripping wet. Shake off excess water (especially with the large fleshy varieties), turn it upside down and let the base dry out before putting it back in its place of residence.

In the warmth of summer, it will need more watering – spray or rinse it two or three times a week (if you keep it outdoors it will dry out faster in the moving air and should be watered four or five times a week). If the leaf edges begin to curl in, its time for an overnight soaking (12–14 hours), followed by shaking and draining as above. Trimming away any brown, dried or injured (bent) leaves won't harm the plant. Of course, the best water for air plants is rain water. Hang them on the washing line or out of your window during a summer shower, to give them a really good soaking.

Surprises
While they're not generally grown for their flowers, some produce really spectacular blooms. Plants can also produce offsets (called pups), so can bulk up into fantastic colonies. Often the original plant will die after blooming. Wait until it has shrivelled up before trimming it off the colony.

SHARE ALERT

If more than one new plant has formed, pups can be separated when about two-thirds the size of the mother plant.

Air plants grow naturally on trees and rocks and even telegraph wires – as seen opposite in Venezuela (photo: Andreas Groeger) – so you have free reign to choose how to display them

Charming

———

Do you take tea in a china teacup, while you curl
up with a 1930s detective novel? Do you wrap
gifts with tissue paper and ribbon? Does your bed
linen have a high thread count? Are you likely
to break out into songs from the shows? My dear,
I think you might be charming.

Cheerful, dainty but resilient, often very fragrant,
the plants in this section have been cultivated
in European gardens for centuries. Between them,
they provide colour and grace throughout the
seasons – bright jewels in the depths of winter,
pretty clusters in the riot of summer.

**Primroses and relatives / violas and pansies /
pinks and carnations / African violets / cyclamen**

Who knew? Auriculas are the delightful offspring of the
stinking primrose and the mountain cowslip

Primroses and their relatives

Primrose / polyanthus / cowslip / auricula

Why grow them? Ask a child to draw a flower and they'll come up with something close to a primrose. These pretty long-flowering low-growing plants brighten up pots and window boxes even in the dark days of late winter. The primrose, its relatives and their cultivars are easy-to-grow plants that flower for months on end, year after year.

What's the story? The primrose (*Primula vulgaris*) is a plant of European hedgerows and open woodlands (and, in recent times, motorway embankments!), where it can carpet the ground with its pretty blossoms. Pink primroses can be found in nature and gardeners over the centuries have drawn out a great range of colours – from true blue and purple to orange and scarlet. The colour range is just as broad in the polyanthus, which is a cross between the primrose and its cousin the cowslip (*Primula veris*) and bears many flowers on a single stem. As primroses and polyanthus are frost hardy, they can be planted out in the autumn, ready to flower at the first hint of spring.

What they like Sun or light shade.

What they loathe Drought.

How to grow them Outside. Plant in autumn or early spring, ensuring the crown (where the leaves emerge) is level with the soil surface. Water regularly, as soon as the first couple of centimetres of soil feels dry. Remove any yellowing leaves and snip off the flowers as each one finishes to encourage more to emerge. Primroses make lovely cut flowers – bring them indoors and make a posy for a tiny vase or egg cup.

Also look out for Auriculas are another lovely primrose relative, with upright clusters of distinctive and delightful flowers. The fine detail of auricula blooms is best appreciated by growing single plants in terracotta pots (19th-century fans displayed them in 'auricula theatres' against black backgrounds to heighten the drama). Some auriculas have a powdery white 'farina' on their buds, flowers and leaves, giving them a pretty, frosted look. Auriculas are a cross between the yellow mountain cowslip (*Primula auricula*) and the deep pink stinking primrose (*Primula hirsuta*) that appeared in gardens in the 16th century. Their high mountain origins mean they need sharper drainage than their lowland cousins, so grow them in an equal-parts mix of horticultural grit and multi-purpose compost. Outdoors, in light shade.

Fragrance alert: primroses are said to smell like a mixture of jasmine and wild roses. In truth, they smell like nothing else. Sweet and fresh, like spring.

Above, a bank of wild primroses and violets in southern England (photo: Katherine Price); right, an orange polyanthus picks out the golden eye of the blue forget-me-not

Chirpy cheep cheep

—

Pansy / viola

Why grow them? Cheerful, early blooming outdoor flowers that are lovely complements to spring bulbs such as daffodils and tulips. They come from woodlands and mountains in cool climates, so are very hardy and do well in partial shade. With a little bit of care, they can flower right through to early autumn.

What's the story? European gardeners have been developing violas and pansies over centuries.

Garden pansies (*Viola tricolor* var. *hortensis*) are descended from the diminutive heartsease and people were mad for them in the 19th century, thanks to the craze for colourful flowerbeds that changed with the seasons. They have big fancy blooms that are out of scale with their foliage, and a well-defined blotch, or eye, in the middle of each five-petalled flower.

Garden violas come from two European species, the mountain violet (*Viola lutea*) and the horned violet (*Viola cornuta*). The plants are more dwarf and compact and produce many small pretty flowers over a long period, making them more weather resistant than the fresh-faced pansy, whose showy flowers can spoil in heavy rain.

How to grow them

Outdoors, in windowboxes, pots and as a foil for larger plants in big containers in sun or part shade. Plant them in multi-purpose compost in containers that are at least 30 cm (12 in) deep. Deadhead regularly to prolong flowering (snipping out the spent flowers and stems) and give them a light trim and tidy all over in July. In early autumn, cut them back to 5 cm (2 in) tall to encourage fresh new growth to see them through the winter. Keep well watered in hot, dry weather and if growing in pots, apply a liquid feed regularly.

Fragrance alert: the most common scent is honey, but viola fragrances range from citrus and cloves to vanilla custard.

PS The name pansy comes from the French *pensée*, meaning thought, as the flower was a symbol of remembrance. But in Shakespeare's play *A Midsummer Night's Dream*, heartsease causes chaos when its juice is used as a love potion (do not try this at home).

Opposite page, if ever a plant could be said to have a cheeky character, it would be the showy pansy; left, violas are almost as cute, but more weather resistant and they flower for a longer time

Cottage garden

Pink carnation / busy Lizzie / snapdragon

Why grow them? With lacy prettiness and spicy fragrance, pinks create a cottage garden in a pot. The wild species were grown in ancient Greece for their striking colours and delicate frills. Wild pinks (*Dianthus plumarius*) and wild carnations (*Dianthus caryophyllus*) are herbaceous species from the mountains and meadows of Europe and Asia. These species are the parents of garden pinks – they form evergreen mounds of blue- or grey-green slender foliage and long-lasting single or double flowers with 'pinked' petals, in a range of colours and patterns, and 10–45 cm (4–18 in) tall.

What they like Full sun and a well-drained growing medium.

How to grow them Outdoors, in window boxes or raised pots, so you can bury your nose in their sweet clove-scented flowers. Deadhead regularly to keep the blooms coming.

'The first plant that inspired me was a snapdragon. My grandma used to pick snapdragon flowers when I was really young and played with them, pretending they were actual little snapping dragons. I still love the plants for their vibrant flower colours and – as I learned later – if you look closely at the seedheads they look like little skulls.'

Rebecca Hilgenhof, tender plants specialist, Kew

─────── SHARE ALERT ───────

Take cuttings of non-flowering stems in summer.

Also look out for more old-world charm, with these two traditional favourites:

Busy Lizzies (*Impatiens*) – the tutti fruttis of container plants, with jewel-like colours and flowers that keep coming all summer long. Unlike many bright floriferous plants, the traditional busy Lizzy (*Impatiens walleriana*) and its cultivars are happiest in moist shade, which mimics the shady wetlands of its natural habitat in eastern Africa. The New Guinea impatiens (*Impatiens hawkeri*) comes from the plant paradise of New Guinea, a large tropical island in the south-west Pacific. It grows in mountain forests and its cultivars are more tolerant of partial sun. See pictures on pages 143 and 159.

Snapdragons (*Antirrhinum majus*) grow in rocky places in south-west Europe and their brilliant free-flowering garden relatives love rich well-drained soil in full sun. Grow them from seed and deadhead regularly to keep them flowering at full tilt. According to a book published in 1943 by Heinrich Marzell, there are more than 100 different common names for snapdragons across the German-speaking world, which just goes to show what engaging little plants they are.

Cottage garden charm: exuberant snapdragon, left, and dainty pink

Indoor charmers

African violet / florist's cyclamen

Why grow them? Intense flower colour and deep-green velvety leaves make the African violet a sophisticated subject for a bright windowsill. Bring them right up to date in a ceramic pot with a strong contemporary design and use them as a table arrangement if you're feeling really posh.

What's the story? African violets (*Saintpaulia ionantha*) are not related to violets, but the first plants to be introduced to Europe from East Africa were the same deep purple as the sweet violet, hence the common name. They come from cloud forests, where they grow in high humidity on mossy rocks in light shade. A close cousin, and just as pretty, is the Cape primrose (*Streptocarpus rexii*), the parent of some fantastic cultivars. Cape primroses need very similar care, with just a little more warmth.

What they like Bright, indirect light, moderate warmth and humidity.

What they loathe Overwatering, direct sun and water on their leaves.

How to grow them Indoors on a bright windowsill, where the temperature is fairly consistent (so not in a draughty hall). Avoid direct sunlight. Plant them in free-draining compost in pots that are about half the diameter of the leaf rosette – constricted roots makes them flower better. As rock dwellers they have shallow roots, so give them shallow pots, no deeper than 10 cm (4 in). Let the compost dry out between thorough waterings and don't leave the pot standing in water. In winter, when central heating dries the atmosphere, raise the humidity by standing the pot on a dish of pebbles that are kept moist. If the leaves turn pale and curl in winter, the plant is too cold. Bring it into a warmer room – you're likely to spend more time there too.

SHARE ALERT

Propagate African violets; cut a healthy leaf and 2cm stem from a plant and push it into a pot filled with moist compost. Seal in a plastic bag to maintain humidity. Keep in a bright spot out of direct sunlight and in 2 to 3 months you will have babies!

Also look out for exquisite nodding flowers with twisting, reflexed petals in all shades of pink, as well as red and pure white, sitting above beautifully patterned leaves. This is the florist's cyclamen.

What's the story? Although they're related to the primrose, it's hard to see any similarities. Florist's cyclamen (*Cyclamen persicum*) originate in southern Turkey, Syria, Lebanon, Jordan and Israel, where they grow on rocky hillsides. In winter they produce white or soft pink flowers with a deep pink zone at the base of each petal – blooms of such loveliness that they must seem like minor miracles in such harsh environments. They grow from firm rounded tubers – an adaptation that allows them to survive dormant underground through hot dry summers. These tubers can live for decades, growing to 30 cm (1 ft) in diameter.

What they like Bright, indirect light. A dry dormant period in summer.

What they loathe Waterlogged soil.

How to grow them Inside, on a bright cool windowsill, *Cyclamen persicum* cultivars will flower all winter. Give them a soil-based, free-draining compost, letting it dry out between waterings. When the flowers stop coming and the leaves turn yellow, stop watering and put them outside in a sheltered place for the summer. Repot them in autumn, resume watering and watch them spring into action.

PS There are some lovely cyclamen for outdoor growing too. Try *Cyclamen coum*, which flowers from winter to spring, and autumn-flowering *Cyclamen hederifolium* in partial shade.

Far left, mimic the humidity of the African violet's native cloud forest by sitting its pot on a dish of wet pebbles; above left, the Florist's cyclamen flowers all winter; outdoors, grow *Cyclamen coum*, seen on the right flowering in its native woodland habitat in the Republic of Georgia (photo: Richard Wilford).

Retro

———

Do you wallow in the riches of the past?
The brocades and flock wallpaper of the age
of Empire? The pretty domesticity of the 1930s?
The groovy lateral living and block colours
of the 1960s and 70s?

The plants in this section have all had their
15 minutes of fame (or decades of demand),
but have since been taken for granted. Fickle
fashion makes us forget why these plants were
hugely popular. Time for a second look, especially
if you tend towards the long view. An instant
hit of nostalgia.

Aspidistra / fuchsia / spider plant / Swiss cheese plant

Fuchsia flowers, like ballerinas

Shady past

Aspidistra / mother-in-law's tongue

Why grow them? The glossy dark green leathery leaves of aspidistra (*Aspidistra elatior*) bring tropical glamour to the shadiest corner of your home, pictured right. The aspidistra's ability to survive in dim, polluted situations made it a must-have in the hallways of 'respectable' boarding houses of the 19th century, and it often features in the stilted photographic portraits of the time. This slow-growing plant's a keeper – rumour has it that it can reach 50 years of age or even more! Imagine having such a fine, undemanding companion on life's journey.

What's the story? It grows under the dense tree canopy in the subtropical forests of Taiwan and southern Japan, so has evolved to deal with deep shade and little water. As a result, in cultivation it will tolerate shade and neglect (hence its common name, cast iron plant), though a little care goes a long way as far as glossiness goes. In Japan, its leaves have traditionally been cut up and used to separate food in bento and osechi lunch boxes. It is related to lily-of-the-valley (*Convallaria*) – look closely, you'll see the resemblance – but grows three times as tall, to 60 cm (2 ft).

What it likes Shade, and an occasional wipe-down of those lovely leaves to get rid of any dust.

What it loathes Direct sunlight, root disturbance and overwatering.

How to grow Indoors, in any level of shade although light shade is best, in a cool (temperature not style) place, such as a hallway. It can also be grown outside in a sheltered spot that doesn't get colder than -5°C (23°F) – or you can wheel it out, like an elderly relative, to a shady position for the summer. Grow

---

SHARE ALERT

When it's time to re-pot, you can divide an aspidistra by cutting off pieces of rhizome (the thick horizontal root) with at least two leaves growing from each piece. Pot them up, water them in and give them away!

in soil-based compost and water freely in summer, feeding once a month and ensuring the compost doesn't become waterlogged. There's no need for high levels of humidity. Ease off on the watering from October to March. Don't repot until the roots are attempting to escape from the bottom of the container. When you do repot, you could divide the plant and share.

Also look out for Mother-in-law's tongue (*Sanseviera trifasciata*) – another handsome evergreen foliage plant forming dense clumps from a creeping rhizome, pictured left. Its stiff narrow leaves, which can grow up to 1.5 m (5 ft) tall, are dark green with light grey-green cross-banding or variegated with stripy leaf margins. Treat it just like aspidistra.

Swing era

—

Fuchsia / spider plant / spiderwort

Why grow them? For the glamour of 1950s *haute couture* or the big skirts and bobby socks of swing and twist, look no further than the fuchsia. Flowering in profusion from summer to autumn, their flouncy pendent blooms sometimes veer into pantomime-dame territory.

What's the story? Most fuchsias come from South America. Their flower colours are classic welcome signs for their hummingbird pollinators, which hover under their hanging flowers to feed on their nectar. Fuchsias were first brought to Europe from the Caribbean in the late 17th century and were at the peak of popularity in the grand houses of the 19th century, only later being adopted by the *hoi polloi* for bright suburban gardens.

What they like Fresh air and bright light, with protection from the sun during the hottest part of the day.

What they loathe Waterlogged soil and hard frosts.

How to grow them Outdoors in summer, in hanging baskets or window boxes – anywhere that gives you an eyeful of their exuberant flowers. Grow them in a rich soil-based potting compost or multi-purpose compost and water well. Many fuchsias don't tolerate hard frosts, so keep them somewhere sheltered in winter and cut them back in spring to stimulate new growth.

Surprises The purple fruits of all fuchsias are edible, although some are tastier than others. Apparently the best-flavoured species is *Fuchsia splendens*, with a citrus and black pepper flavour. Make into jam or add to salads for extra zing.

Spider plants, pictured right, had their moment of glory in the 1970s, the decade of craft and home-brewing, when they hung around the house and yard and fire escape in macramé slings of various shades of beige. Get that layered look with a twist of contemporary colour by using bright fibres and glazed pots.

What's the story The spider plant (*Chlorophytum comosum*) was the austerity plant of the 1970s – easy to grow and easy to share. This evergreen perennial comes from South Africa, where it is found in the undergrowth of forested slopes, on flat terrain and on cliffs. It forms large colonies thanks to its means of reproduction – throwing out slender arching shoots with tiny spiderettes at their ends, which root where they touch the ground.

How to grow them Indoors, either hanging or on a raised shelf, in a bright cool room (see picture on page 33), avoiding direct sunlight in the middle of the day. Grow in free-draining compost (two parts multi-purpose compost to one part vermiculite). Water well and let the compost dry out between waterings. Spider plants are happy in confined quarters, so repot only when the large fleshy roots are highly visible and watering is difficult.

Also look out for Trailing spiderwort (*Tradescantia pallida* and *Tradescantia zebrina*) from the Americas, with sprawling stems and handsome leaves and flowers.

PS These plants are toxic to pets and people – double reason to hang them up somewhere out of reach.

——— **SHARE ALERT** ———

Detach spiderettes from the mother spider plant and pin them to the surface of a fresh pot of compost. Keep them well watered. Once they've rooted, share!

Opposite, 1950s-style silhouette of the fuchsia flower; above left, get the 70s vibe with the sprawling spiderwort and, above right, the stripey spider plant (hanging out here with an airplant and a maidenhair fern)

Feeling groovy

Swiss cheese plant / rubber plant

Why grow them? Get the mid-century modern style with a Swiss cheese plant (*Monstera deliciosa*). Which interiors or fashion magazine from the 1960s doesn't have one of these divas completely upstaging the model draped across the G Plan couch? These plants work for the dramatic among you too – monster by name, monster by nature, but in a Big Friendly Giant kind of a way – growing to more than 3 m (10 ft) tall, even in the confines of an apartment in the northern hemisphere.

What's the story? This evergreen vine scrambles through tropical rainforests in Central America. It is cultivated for its edible fruits, which taste like a cross between a banana and a pineapple. The young plants have small entire leaves, without holes and lobes, but as they grow they develop their characteristic Swiss cheese holeyness, so they don't get shredded by the heavy storms that batter the tropical forest.

What they like Bright light, high humidity and free-draining soil.

'The plant that got me into plants was the Swiss cheese plant! I remember thinking it looked so completely different from any plant I'd seen before. It's still one of my favourites and I have two at home.'

Chris Brown, student gardener, Kew

Big plants with big characters: the bold glossy foliage of the Swiss cheese plant, far right, and the rubber plant, right

What they loathe Direct sun and deep shade. They rarely flower when grown indoors.

How to grow them Indoors, in a warm bright room, but out of direct sunlight. Grow in free-draining compost (two parts multi-purpose compost to one part vermiculite) or soil-based compost. Between waterings, allow the top 2 cm (3/4 in) of compost to dry out. Train them up a pole to imitate the way they grow in the wild, where they attach to other plants by means of their aerial roots. Ideally use a moss pole (a column of coir that the aerial roots can dig in to), which can be sprayed with water to keep the humidity high around the leaves. Repot every few years and top-dress in between (remove the top few centimetres of old compost and replace with fresh compost). If your plant gets too big, trim it to size (see *Pruning and deadheading* on page 230).

Also look out for Rubber plant (*Ficus elastica*) – more monstrous than the *Monstera*, this Asian tree grows to 40 m (130 ft) in the wild, but the hybrid houseplants don't get too carried away, producing beautiful structured leaves.

Structural

Clean lines and order are the watchwords of your space. No hippy-dippy swirling colours or clutter. Modern, smart and balanced. So revel in the rhythmic patterns and geometry of these structural plants. They come in many shapes and sizes, remaining fairly static all year round. You won't come back from a trip to find they've taken over. They do flower occasionally, but that's not why we grow them.

Why do plants evolve with different structures? If they all need the same thing – light, water, humidity, nutrients – why don't they all have the same form? Because they don't exist in a vacuum. Different topography, climate, other plants, predators and so on, all play their part. These structural plants have all evolved to withstand seasonal water shortages... and, if they're spiny, goats!

Houseleeks and family / cacti / aloes and family

Feast for the eye: agaves, cacti and a haworthia; overleaf, pelargoniums, Arabian jasmine, cactus, aloes and echeveria

Houseleeks and family

Houseleek / stonecrop / aeonium / echeveria / jade plant

Why grow them? Houseleeks form mats of succulent rosettes in an incredible range of colours, from lime green to mushroom grey, with wine-red along the way. In addition, some of them have dense spidery webbing that gives them a frosted look.

What's the story? They grow in crevices and on rocks in the mountains of Europe, North Africa and the Caucasus, some even above the tree line. Their rosettes persist through the winter, as their Latin name suggests: *Sempervivum* meaning always living. Old medicinal- and witch-plants, they are linked in folklore with Thor, the Norse god of thunder, and people believed that having them growing on your roof would protect your house from lightning.

What they like Fresh air and sunshine. Their mountain origins mean they are frost hardy and drought resistant. They can take intense summer sunshine and pounding thunderstorms. In short, they're bomb proof.

What they loathe Sitting in the cold and wet for any period of time.

'The plants I wouldn't be without at home are succulents. My echeveria had never flowered in ten years, but this summer I moved it outside onto the balcony for the first time. It obviously loved the south-facing white wall and has produced flowers for the first time.'

Maia Ross, herbaceous perennial specialist, Kew

How to grow them Outdoors. Give them a free-draining soil-based compost (one part compost to one part grit) and a collar of grit on the surface to make sure water doesn't sit around their necks. They aren't needy plants and don't require feeding. Repot them every few years, and the fresh compost will give them all the food they need, as well as some fresh air for their roots.

Surprises They produce the occasional crazy cartoon of a flower. The thing about flowering is that once they do it, they die. Which is not as drastic as it sounds. Just remove the dead rosette and the others will grow to fill the space.

Houseleek relatives
Outdoors all year, in sun or partial shade: Stonecrop (*Sedum*) – these mainly northern hemisphere succulents love sun and dry soil, but will also tolerate winter cold, as long as they're in a free-draining spot.

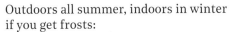

Outdoors all summer, indoors in winter
if you get frosts:
Aeonium – mostly from the Canary Islands,
these subtropical plants like sandy soil
and tolerate drought, so they're great for
hot dry corners of the yard (see page 146).
Echeveria – from semi-desert regions
of Central America, with beautiful flowers
to match their wonderful rosettes.
Jade plant (*Crassula ovata*) – a slow-growing
shrub from South Africa that can eventually
reach 2 m (7 ft) tall! (see page 196)

SHARE ALERT

Houseleeks are easy-peasy to propagate.
Each rosette puts out small offsets, or baby
rosettes, on slender stems above ground.
These root where they touch the soil.
Detach them, pot up and share.

Opposite, mountain houseleek flowering on rock outcrops in the
Swiss Alps (photo: Joanne Everson); top left, fascinating clusters of
houseleek rosettes; bottom left, an unusual stonecrop with a woody
stem; right, succulent blue foliage of echeveria, a beautiful, less
hardy American cousin of the houseleek

Prickly customers

Cacti

Why grow them? Nothing changes a space like a cactus. Their fascinating forms bring texture and colour, and they also have strong personalities – not just prickly ones – as if they're just waiting to strike up a conversation. (Why not try it?) They include slender fluted columns, plump globose clusters, solitary obese types, and branching trees straight out of wild-west comic strips. Most of them are covered in spines, some with wispy shrouds of silver hairs or stiff feathery plumes. And when they flower, they do it magnificently.

What's the story? Most cacti come from the semi-desert regions of South and Central America and south-west United States, although a few species come from forests. Those from arid habitats are adapted to hot, dry environments. One of the key adaptations is a lack of foliage. Leaves increase a plant's surface area, which leads to greater water loss. That's a no-no in a desert.

So if they don't have leaves, where do they do their photosynthesis? Simple. In their stems. Instead of leaves, cacti have spines, which protect the plants from grazing animals but also help to conserve water. They trap air near the surface of the cactus, raising the humidity, which suppresses water loss. The spines also provide some shade and catch dew and fog, which then drips onto the ground to be absorbed by the plant's shallow roots. In most cacti, the stem is the main water store.

Cacti produce a stunning diversity of brilliant flowers, and are pollinated by insects and birds (especially hummingbirds). Some are even pollinated by bats, particularly those tree-like species scattered across large areas of semi-desert. Bat-pollinated flowers normally open in the evening and at night, are white or green, produce lots of nectar and emit a musty smell that beckons bats from miles around.

Garden centres often sell plants labelled simply as 'cactus', but there is a huge range of species with wonderful names. Look out for *Cephalocereus*, *Cereus*, *Cylindropuntia*, *Echinocereus*, *Echinopsis*, *Gymnocalycium*, *Mammillaria*, *Notocactus*, *Opuntia*, *Pilosocereus*, *Rebutia* and *Trichocereus*. If they are widely available, they are likely to be easy to grow.

What they like Dry air, bright light and protection from very hot direct sun.

What they loathe Cold, wet compost.

How to grow them Indoors on a sunny or bright windowsill with good air circulation. Grow them in an open free-draining mixture of two parts soil-based compost to one part grit. During the growing season (April to September), water them freely with rainwater, allowing the compost to dry out between waterings, and feed once a month. In early autumn, reduce watering and give them cool night-time temperatures down to 10°C (50°F) to encourage a period of rest.

Also look out for Mistletoe cactus (*Rhipsalis*), Christmas cactus (*Schlumbergera*) and Easter cactus (*Hatiora*), which are different, with very reduced spines (or even no spines) and flattened stems in sections. They come from forests where they are epiphytes, growing on other plants and rocks, and often have arching and trailing shapes, making them great subjects for hanging baskets. They have very different needs to their spiny cactus cousins: morning sun and afternoon shade, as well as humidity. Like their cousins, they enjoy very reduced water in winter. See pictures on pages 170, 188, 189 and 197.

Cacti pseuds – several species of *Euphorbia* (the spurge family) are sold as handsome pseudo-cacti with swollen columnar or globose stems, complete with spikes. But if you look carefully, you can see that the thorn is not a distinct spine protruding from an areole (the distinctive feature of cacti). And if you cut a euphorbia, a sticky, milky-white fluid containing latex emerges (which is a skin irritant, so wash it off immediately if you make contact).

Left, barrel cactus growing wild in Arizona, USA; above, saguaro cactus can grow to more than 20 m tall in their native habitat, Arizona, USA (photos: Maia Ross); cacti species showing off their enchanting diversity, far left and top right

Succulent survivors

Aloes and their relatives, haworthias

Why grow them? Bold architectural forms, more upright and spiky than houseleeks, with spines, ridges and patterns on waxy succulent leaves across the green spectrum. They come in many sizes, from a few centimetres across to tree-like species that grow to 3 m (10 ft) tall. They produce clusters of pendent yellow, orange or red tubular flowers.

What's the story? Aloes come from Africa, the Arabian Peninsula and islands of the Indian Ocean. Now extinct in the wild, *Aloe vera* has been used for its healing properties since Egyptian times. Aloes are pollinated by non-hovering sunbirds and, as a result of their co-evolution, aloe flowers are carried on rigid stalks that make perfect perches.

What they like Bright light and restricted water.

What they loathe Frost.

How to grow them Just like cacti – indoors on a sunny or bright windowsill with good air circulation. Grow them in an open free-draining mixture of two parts soil-based compost to one part grit. Most aloes like cool dry winter conditions, so cut back on watering from autumn to spring. A handful – including the spiralling *Aloe polyphylla* from the mountains of Lesotho – can be grown outside all year round in regions with milder winters.

Marvellous aloe relatives Haworthias are small sharp-suited succulents, mostly from sandy, rocky regions of South Africa. They have an intriguing range of shapes and characters, some with very hard, ridged dark green leaves, others softer, rounder, with translucent 'windows' in their leaves that let sunlight into internal photosynthetic tissues, so they can survive partially buried in the ground. Haworthias are happy in partial shade as they tend to grow under bushes or rock overhangs in their natural habitats. Otherwise, give them the same treatment as their aloe cousins.

'I have always been interested in haworthias – they are compact, interesting to look at and easy to look after. I grow *Haworthia planifolia*, which is really straightforward. And they remind me of home.'

Paul Rees, cacti and succulent specialist, Kew

— SURVIVAL IN THE HARSH DESERT —

Photosynthesis needs light energy, so it happens during the day. It also depends on a good supply of carbon dioxide, which plants take up through open stomata (leaf pores). This leads to water loss, which can be a real problem in hot dry habitats. Cacti and succulents have got around this with an adaptation that allows them to keep their stomata closed during the day. Instead, they open their stomata at night when it's cooler and they don't lose so much water. They collect carbon dioxide, store it as an acid in their cells, then convert it back into carbon dioxide during the day for use in photosynthesis. This adaptation has a suitably sci-fi name – crassulacean acid metabolism. It requires much more energy than standard photosynthesis, which helps to explain the slow growth of cacti and succulents compared to other plants.

Opposite, dry lands of South Africa, where adaptation is critical to survival (photo: Paul Rees); left, *Haworthia pumila* middle with *Haworthia cymbiformis* (below) and *Haworthia attenuata* (top); *Aloe brevifolia* with Arabian jasmine (above) and *Echeveria glauca* (right).

Part Three: Places

Plants have been on a long journey. Over millions of years they have carved out niches for themselves, evolving to make the best out of their habitats and their interactions with the plants and animals that surround them.

Most are adapted to a quite specific range of conditions. They know what they like! But in the end it still comes down to light, heat, water and nutrients.

Think about where you live. How does the sunlight travel around your home as the sun sails across the sky? Do puddles in your yard freeze over in winter? Is there space on a bright shelf in your living room that never gets very warm? Does the wind whip across your balcony at any time of year?

By understanding your indoor and outdoor living spaces, you can replicate your plant's favoured habitat. You can't conjure up the soundscape of the rainforest or the silent reaches of the steppe or the brilliance of the migrating monarch butterflies, but you can recreate the humidity and low light of the tropical forest understorey or the bright, dry stillness of the desert in winter.

Great outdoors

Life, outdoors

Even in the concretiest of concrete jungles, plants find niches. You've no doubt seen the straggly butterfly bush on railway embankments, bright green ferns on shady walls and dandelions waving from cracks in the pavement. Then of course there are the trees, filtering the light and cooling the streets. Birds and insects follow.

Plants transform outdoor spaces, framing your view of the world, welcoming you home. If you have room for just one pot on your doorstep or outside your kitchen window, make it a good one, brimming with life.

The sun may never reach the damp yard at the bottom of the fire escape but there's a fern from a subtropical forest that will love its cool humidity. You may only be able to take it in turns to stand on your tiny balcony but at night the scent from the flowers growing in the pot at your feet reaches every corner of the flat. And when it seems like winter's never going to end there are bulbs popping up in your window box shouting 'Spring!' Whatever your home is like you can get plants. Plants have evolved to thrive in their own specific ecosystems but those very same adaptations mean you can grow them in your space too.

Border auriculas are great for pots or flowerbeds

The yard or town garden

Your yard. It's not so nice. There's a pile of bicycles in various states of repair. The rubbish and recycling bins line up along one wall like drunken soldiers. The concrete is cracked and turning to scree and the sun is like a sledgehammer in summer and barely peeks over the enclosing wall in winter.

Do not despair. This, my friend, is an opportunity.

Even in the starkest space there is light and shade. And you can grow a range of vegetable companions for colour, scent, structure and even food.

Greening the space brings life into it. Birds and predatory insects will start to visit, decimating the population of flies around the bins. You might find that even humans could sit out there on a warm summer evening or sunny winter afternoon.

Carmine-coloured cosmos light up this west-facing courtyard garden

Fifty shades of yard

Think about how your back yard is used. If it's mainly a corridor, then your plants need to be fairly well behaved, so they don't obstruct the walkways. If there's enough space for a table and chairs but not enough for containers on the ground, consider hanging plants from the walls. If there's a bit more space, then you have more decisions to make.

Do you want to grow specimen plants in lots of individual pots? They will need more watering, but the advantage is that you can move them around, bringing the daffodils to the front in their moment of glory, then stashing them behind the tulips as they die down.

Do you want to create mini-gardens in larger containers such as half-barrels and old tin baths? Clever planting means you can have a long season of interest, with different species flowering in succession.

If you have a continental climate, do you just want to green up your yard for the hot summer and turn your back on it throughout the freezing winter?

And how will you get water to your plants? If there's a down pipe channelling rainwater from the roof of the building into the ground, ask your landlord if you can siphon some of that stuff of life into a water butt (the technology is beautifully simple). If watering is a logistical nightmare, heaving watering cans up and down the fire escape, consider plants that tolerate drought, to minimise the effort. Or ask an engineer friend to design a clever lift-and-pulley contraption (and if you ask nicely, she might even install it for you).

Take time to work out how the sun moves around the yard during the day. If the sun is only there in the morning, the yard faces east. If it gets sun all day, it's south facing. And if the sun arrives in the afternoon, then your yard faces west. This may sound like unnecessary detail, but actually there's a limited number of plants that thrive in full summer sun all day long (even the plants of the prairies get shade from each other).

'Look at how backgrounds and colours can affect the impact of your plants. The perfect example of this is the Jardin Majorelle in Morocco with its vivid blue walls. My wife and I have used this blue as a backdrop to our plants for years. First we painted the inside of our balcony with it when we lived in a block of flats and now we've got a garden, we've painted our fences that colour. The blue really helps to accentuate the form and colour of your plants.'

Nick Johnson, tropical and tender plants specialist, Kew

Grow bougainvillea on a sunny windowsill indoors and, when the frosts are over, take it outside for the summer

The sun lovers

Track down some large containers – half-barrels, old tin baths, etc – and fill them with a range of plants that flower at different times through the year. Larger containers hold on to water for longer, which cuts down on watering. But watch out for waterlogging, which very few plants tolerate.

For a succession of brilliant displays from February to May, plant taller daffodil and tulip cultivars in autumn. Water them regularly and thoroughly as soon as their foliage begins to push through the surface of the soil. These hill and mountain dwellers are programmed to take advantage of spring rains, flowering and setting seed before the harsh summer begins. Their leaves harness the sun, recharging their bulbs, which store food and moisture so they can survive underground until the following spring.

They say there's a daisy for every day of the year and most of them are sun lovers, coming from exposed mountain slopes, grasslands and disturbed ground (caused by farming or landslides) around the world. They have fabulous garden relatives and with a soil-based compost and regular feeding, and watering, you can have a daisy display in a container from spring to autumn (see page 72).

Of course, if you're competitive and assiduous, you could grow giant sunflowers (*Helianthus*), for their stupendous flowerheads – allow them to mature and you could be very popular with the seed-eaters among the local bird population.

The yard is a great place for growing cordon tomatoes (the ones you need to train up supports), sheltering them from the wind, but with enough space so that sun can get to each plant and ripen their wonderful fruit. Growbags aren't beautiful but they have been developed with good cropping in mind.

KEW TIP

If you're really short of indoor space, instead of lifting your dahlia tubers after the first frosts, leave them in their pots, insulated with bubblewrap and pushed into a corner of the yard to keep the rain off them.

Grasses

For natural drama, silver grass (*Miscanthus sinensis*), from mountain slopes in China and Japan, will give you a stately display. Its erect green stems bear beautiful golden spiky sprays of flowers that bleach to silvery-white and catch the frost and winter sun.

Opposite, plump juicy cordon tomatoes need space, sun, shelter and lots of food and water; top left, ox-eye daisies, with the old-fashioned ruffles of fragrant pinks (left) and roses; top right, a dahlia's deep purple foliage is a great foil for its orange blooms and for the rusty red of its chrysanthemum cousin, while the arching foliage of silver grass provides a cool contrast to all that hot autumn colour; right, stately sunflowers sizzle in the summer sun (say out loud, repeat)

Drama of light and shade

Plants from forest margins and mountains grow well in places that don't get full sun all day long. And many plant species flower better in a less harsh environment.

Above right, the muted colours of grasses and succulents make good companions in sun and shade; opposite, pale splashes on hosta leaves bring light to a shady corner; above (clockwise from left) elegant fronds of Japanese painted fern, the bold leaves of *Fatsia*, stripey foliage of a sedge, bright starry lily flowers and the robust rhythm of the shield fern; overleaf, Tulipa 'Abu Hassan', Rosa 'Parade Neza'

Large-leaved evergreen plants can make even the dingiest, dampest corner a place of intrigue, with rich textures and colours and light-reflecting foliage. The plants on these pages all come from temperate forests, where they form spreading colonies. So give them humid shade, a soil-based compost and regular watering through the growing season.

Ferns While the male fern (*Dryopteris filix-mas*) can form large colonies in the damp understorey of European and North American woodlands, it also grows on hedge banks and rocks, so can cope with being in a container. With shade and sufficient moisture, its intriguing croziers unfurl and extend as deep green fronds to 1.5 m (5 ft) tall.

Bold foliage The bigger the container, the bigger the plant. And deeper shade means deeper green. From forests on the rocky coasts of southern Japan and Korea, *Fatsia japonica* is a large evergreen shrub that is hardy down to -15°C (5°F). In colder areas, grow it as a houseplant for a tropical effect. It carries its large eight-lobed glossy leaves (*fatsi* is an approximation of the old Japanese word for eight) on sturdy branches and makes instant impact in a shady spot.

They aren't evergreen, but the larger plantain lilies (*Hosta*) offer wonderful variations on the big-leaf theme, with pleats and quilted effects and colours ranging from lime green to dusky blue, sometimes with yellow or white variegation. In nature, they're found in East Asian river valleys and mountains and while they will tolerate morning sun, they grow better in shade.

Succulent structural echeveria cultivars won't survive a frost, but thrive outdoors in summer. In spite of their Mexican origins, their succulent leaves can be scorched by strong sunshine, so place them out of reach of the damaging rays of a summer's afternoon.

It's not surprising that the huge grass family provides us with some stunning plants for partial shade, many of which grow well in containers. Place them where the morning or afternoon sun slants through their foliage, and catches their flowers and seed heads.

Peppermint *Mentha x piperita* is a vigorous hybrid of watermint and spearmint and is best grown in containers to restrict its rapid spread. Keep it well watered (but not waterlogged) in part-shade or shade.

Many of the most dramatic lily *Lilium* species come from forest habitats, so grow well in part or full shade, lighting up dark areas with their large waxy trumpets. Look for Martagon, Oriental or Asiatic lilies. See picture on page 140.

'One of the first plants that caught my attention was *Fatsia*. I thought they looked so tropical, a great foliage addition to any garden. As a bee keeper from an early age, I also realised they are a great late season nectar source.'

Tony Hall, woody plants specialist, Kew

Hang loose

Raise plants up so you can catch an eyeful of their complex flowers or bury your nose in their fragrance. Some plants really can't be appreciated fully unless they are able to flex their trailing limbs or pour from their container in a waterfall of foliage.

If you hang containers from walls and railings, you have to be doubly vigilant about watering. Gravity pulls water straight through the compost and water evaporates from all sides. On the plus side, it's difficult to overwater a hanging plant. But then you need to water a lot in the growing season – every day in high summer – to keep your plants happy. All that watering flushes the nutrients out of the compost too, so you need to add liquid feed regularly (following the instructions of course – too much food makes plants feel bad, just like people).

Sun Trailing petunias produce brilliant floral cascades all summer long. Grow them in baskets hung where they will get at least six hours of sunshine a day. Fed and watered well, these amazing South Americans keep on popping out blooms in crazy colours from late spring until the first frosts. Deadhead them daily as you go to and from home. One of the parent species of our crazy garden petunias comes from rocky outcrops in subtropical South America, which explains why its descendants thrive high up and hot.

Part shade Like pert ballroom dancers, with complex colour ways and nipped-in waists, the flowers of trailing fuchsias can be fully appreciated when they are grown in a hanging basket. There are some marvellous cultivars bred especially to trail. Cultivar names like 'Mrs Popple', 'Auntie Jinks', 'Daisy Bell' and 'Swingtime' capture the cheeky nostalgia of these old-fashioned darlings. The parent

of most cultivars is the wonderful pink and purple *Fuchsia magellanica*, which comes from Chile and Argentina. It grows in forest margins and clearings and is adapted to partial shade, so its descendants grow better in a place that gets sun in the morning and is shaded from the intense light and heat in the afternoon. Now and then, shorten the branches to encourage the plant to stay bushy. Deadhead whenever you pass.

Tuberous begonias (*Begonia* x *tuberhybrida*) produce their exotic brilliant blooms all summer until the first frosts, while the intense colours of dainty cyclamen flowers and their finely patterned leaves are like little miracles in the darker days of autumn and winter. Both plants grow from tubers, so they are able to deal with short periods of drought, making them excellent for hanging baskets. However, for the best displays, keep the begonia well fed and watered.

Above, purple trailing petunias produce cascades of trumpet-shaped flowers, clashing gloriously in full sun with scarlet pelargoniums; opposite, cyclamen are great for hanging baskets and window boxes in part shade or shade and can be planted under shrubs in larger tubs; above left, fuchsias deserve close attention to appreciate their complex dancing blooms

Balcony or terrace

———

Ah, the balcony! Ah, the terrace! Views towards
the mountains or the sea. An earnest lover serenading
you from the street below. Breakfast in the cool quiet,
before the day begins. Drinking hot chocolate
on a crisp winter's day looking out over the trees.
Playing music as the sun sets over the lake.

The reality can be rather less romantic. A windy
platform with an imposing view of the neighbouring
apartment block. Noise and fumes from the traffic
in the street below. Visits from pigeons and seagulls,
which soon lose their novelty. Either no escape from
the hot sun or never a glimpse of it.

But this smidgeon of outside space can be transformed
into a lovely retreat by plants. They filter noise,
provide shelter from the sun and wind, brighten up
shade and surround you with fragrance. They can give
you privacy and peace in the urban hurly-burly.
Or create a laid-back venue for *al fresco* socialising.

The plants on these pages are generally smaller
than the suggestions for the yard, but could
equally well be grown there.

Shouty plants for sunny places: pelargonium and dahlia

All the world's a stage

Tending to plants on your balcony is to play out a little bit of your life on a public stage. The amount of time you spend out there will depend on how comfortable you feel – this isn't just about being observed, but also about which way the balcony faces, how much built-in screening it has, whether it's in a wind tunnel or a sheltered courtyard.

A very exposed balcony several storeys up gives you a lot of light and air, but it also limits the range of plants you can grow. Drying winds can scorch foliage and suck containers dry. Storms can rip plants from the supports you've painstakingly trained them up. Less hardy plants will suffer in the frost. But get your choices right and a light airy balcony can be stuffed full of plants. And the more you have, the more they will filter the winds and shelter each other from extreme weather, creating a benevolent microclimate that is good for them and lovely for you.

By contrast, a balcony overhung by the balcony upstairs, or set into the building and only open on one side, will be very sheltered. It could get hot and humid if it faces south, or cool and damp if it faces north, and this will again affect the plants you can grow.

'Dahlias are one of my favourite flowers, and one of the first I grew as a child thanks to the influence of my grandfather. One of the reasons that I like giant dahlias is that they remind me of my mother's fabulously lurid floral 70's Nelbarden rubber swimming hats... I use medium-sized dahlias in Kew's bedding schemes as dot plants, and grow giant ones at home for cut flowers – you can't fail to be impressed with a flower measuring over 30 cm across!'

Greg Redwood, tender plants specialist, Kew

Opposite, a riot of colour from pinwheel petunias and crazy cockscombs, with the chocolate foliage of coleus, golden sunflowers and a pink busy Lizzy in the background; right (clockwise from bottom left), a hot corner, with pink busy Lizzy on the lower step, red bedding or wax begonia, a red dahlia with deep purple foliage, a large shrubby red fuchsia and the blue flower spikes of a salvia cultivar

And how are you going to get all your containers, plants and compost onto the balcony in the first place? A purpose-built balcony will have been constructed to carry a lot of weight, but check with your landlord if you're appropriating a flat roof for your gardening ambitions – it might not be too sturdy.

Degrees of exposure

—

Your balcony might be a wild and open place or a more sheltered spot, away from desiccating winds. Whichever it is, if the sun shines all day your plants need to be robust to survive the scorching light of a summer afternoon.

Those curious carnivorous pitcher plants (*Sarracenia*) have evolved in the bogs of the south-eastern United States where there is little tree cover, so they can take full sun. Pitcher plants need to be kept waterlogged, and will suffer if you give them tap water (which is usually alkaline). Use cooled water from the kettle or, better still, find an ingenious way of catching and storing rainwater – this is the only plant on the balcony that cannot do without it.

Sun and air Keep your herbs close at hand. Release their fragrance by brushing past them or bruising a sprig between your fingers. Coming from rocky Mediterranean hillsides, culinary herbs such as rosemary (*Rosmarinus*), thyme (*Thymus*) and sage (*Salvia*) grow well in sunny airy spaces. As does lavender (*Lavandula*).

The smaller painted daisies (*Tanacetum*) from the Caucasus, African daisies (*Osteospermum*) and blue marguerites (*Felicia amelloides*) from South Africa, and marguerites (*Argyranthemum*) from the Canary Islands complement the herbs in a naturalistic planting, and your balcony will be buzzing with pollinating insects.

For structure, add smaller grasses like tufty blue fescue (*Festuca glauca*), wispy feather grass (*Stipa barbata*) or fountain grass (*Pennisetum orientale*).

From exposed mountains, houseleeks (*Sempervivum*) are extremely hardy but also tolerate hot sun and neglect (so they're very forgiving if you're away a lot), always looking sharp and structural, with their spreading mats of intriguing rosettes. Raise their containers up and lose yourself in their complex geometries.

Spring elegance comes from daffodils (*Narcissus*) and tulips (*Tulipa*), which evolved in similar rocky open habitats. A bright breezy balcony is the place for smaller species and cultivars to mount their dazzling spring displays.

Sun and shelter Those hot crops from South America – chillies and tomatoes – will appreciate shelter from the wind and intense sunlight to ripen their bright fruits. Chilli peppers grow well outdoors if you have a hot sunny spot and the restricted space of the balcony is more suited to smaller bush tomatoes (that don't need training, just lots of food and water) or cultivars that trail their tempting fruits from a hanging basket.

Revitalise a jaded breakfast on the balcony with blasts of colour from tropical cockscombs (*Celosia*) and South American petunias (*Petunia*). Their parents evolved on sun-drenched stony slopes, so they'll take all the sun you can give them. See picture on page 136.

Opposite, get the natural look with spiky blue fescue, perennial purple wallflower, French lavender and scabious; above, from the Canary Islands, the tree aeonium with its dramatic rosettes and marguerite with its pretty daisy flowers can take all the sun can throw at them - as can pheasant's tail grass (left) and a bowl of mixed houseleeks and saxifrages (front)

Seeking shelter

If your balcony only gets sun early or late in the day and is protected from harsh winds, then let plants from forest clearings bring you leafy and floral loveliness

Grow lettuces in part shade to prevent flowering (otherwise known as bolting) and you can keep on cropping them all season.

Fuchsias are plants from forest clearings, so give them shelter from the hottest sun and from drying winds and they'll reward you with complex dangling blooms all summer.

Spring charm comes from polyanthus (*Primula*), with bright flowers held in big clusters on slender stalks above textured leaves. Plant them with forget-me-nots (*Myosotis*) to remind you of sun-dappled hedgerows and woodland margins of the countryside.

'I've always got one or two chilli plants on the go. I like the idea of growing my own food and they're small and ornamental, so they're good even if you haven't got much space. Plus they are a horticultural challenge – you need to start them from seed early in the year and give them a bit of attention to get a good crop. I try different varieties, aiming for the perfect heat between can't-feel-your-mouth and flavoursome.'

Joe Archer, kitchen gardener, Kew

Above, lettuces; opposite left, this vibrant deep pink busy Lizzy originates in the mountain forests of New Guinea and tolerates partial sun; right, orange polyanthus, blue forget-me-not and wood melick, a shade-loving grass

Shade Busy Lizzies (*Impatiens*) bring brilliant colours to shady places. There are two types in the nursery trade: the eastern African busy Lizzy (*Impatiens walleriana*) hails from shady wetlands so its cultivars are happiest in moist shade, while cultivars of New Guinea impatiens (*Impatiens hawkeri*) can tolerate partial sun, reflecting their origins in mountain forests.

Naturally, forest grasses are adapted to shade. Wood melick (*Melica uniflora*) is native to shady deciduous forests, from Scandinavia south to Turkey and Iran. A small grass growing to 60 cm (2 ft), it has lovely arching panicles of flowers and then seeds that catch the light like sprays of water droplets. There is a variegated cultivar with fresh green and white striped leaves. Two beautiful grasses that are stunning in shade are *Hakonechloa macra* and *Carex morrowii*, both from the wooded mountains of Japan. Their variegated cultivars light up dark areas with arching clumps of yellow and green stripy foliage.

Smaller ferns soften and brighten a shady corner. The brilliant green hart's tongue fern (*Asplenium scolopendrium*) has its origins growing among rocks, meaning it is happy in a raised container or hanging basket. It can also be grown indoors. See page 210.

'Busy Lizzies were the first plants that caught my attention. My grandma had a long walkway to her front door from the street, and they were planted all along it in summer. She would send me out to deadhead them. I loved it.'

Chrissie Mulrain, perennial plant specialist, Kew

Doorstep

Welcome home or bon voyage!

The front door is the portal between your private and public worlds. Here on your doorstep you can grow plants that mark the seasons – even if you live in a totally urban place, you salute the passing year and keep a torch burning for the big wide natural world out there. Grow plants that welcome you home with cheerful blossom or delight passers-by with their intricate forms. Grow plants that waft fragrance down the road. And be prepared to chat to neighbours about your vegetable friends – nothing brings people together like plants.

Streetwise plants

Other people don't care about your plants as much as you do. They haven't taken the time to get to know them. They don't realise you've grown that handsome clump of grass from seed or that you've managed to keep the pelargonium going for four years by taking cuttings or that the tulip bulbs were a present from your great aunt. So plants on the doorstep need to be robust enough to deal with the rough and tumble of the street.

Doorstep plants also need to be relatively well behaved (the person delivering a parcel will not appreciate having to negotiate the thorny tendrils of the rambling rose) and stable, so your flatmate doesn't knock over the pot whenever she brings her bike indoors. The container should be slightly raised, so it drains well and also deters the cheeky dog that trots past every day from using it as a latrine (and on that subject, don't grow your edibles on your front doorstep!). Make sure the container is well stocked with plants or mulched, so the local cats can't use it as a daybed or worse (pesky cats!).

Doorstep in sun If your doorstep gets sun all day, try elegant tulips from the hot dry steppes of Asia and the Middle East. Or trumpet the spring with daffodils from the sunny meadows of Europe and North Africa.

Aeoniums make handsome summer sentries, as long as you return them indoors at the first hint of frost. They evolved on arid hillsides of the Canary Islands and North Africa and are well suited to occasional neglect in the watering department when you're away.

Later in the season, get a summer sunburst from the daisies – marguerites (*Argyranthemum frutescens*) (see page 139), also from the Canary Islands, and autumn colour from chrysanthemums (see page 127).

Autumn and winter are the high seasons for grasses, their seedheads and foliage bleaching elegantly as the year draws to a close.

Doorstep in part sun Drench your visitors in fragrance in early spring from the large bright clusters of trumpet-shaped flowers that make the hyacinth (*Hyacinthus orientalis*) so celebrated around the world. These bulbs originate on rocky cliffs in Turkey, Syria and the Lebanon at altitudes of up to 2,500 m (8,200 ft), and in order to flower they need winter dormancy brought on by the cold. Growing them in part shade prolongs their flowering (see page 144).

The lovely dancing flowers of the fuchsia will mesmerise the neighbour's cat all summer long. Many fuchsias are derived from *Fuchsia magellanica*, a species from forest clearings in southern South America, so they prefer shelter from the hottest sun and can deal with several degrees of frost, in spite of their tender appearance (see page 102).

Opposite, striking succulent rosettes of the purple aeonium will stop passers by in their tracks; below, cyclamen-flowered daffodils trumpet the spring

'I would never be without Mexican feather grass (*Nassella tenuissima* – formerly *Stipa tenuissima*). I brush my hand through its soft foliage every time I go in and out of the front door. It glows in the summer evening light.'

Ed Ikin, landscape and horticulture specialist, Kew

Left and below, hostas provide handsome foliage for a doorstep in dappled shade; opposite, bring the wild woodland to your door with fragrant primroses, lily-of-the-valley and sweet violet, surrounding the bugle's purple spike

Doorstep in shade Greet your guests with the handsome quilted foliage of hostas (*Hosta*). From rocky places in the Far East, they do well in containers, which help to keep them out of reach of slugs and snails. Just make sure they're well watered and give the surface of the compost a thick mulch to hold in moisture. Hostas retreat underground in winter, so you can plant snowdrop (*Galanthus*) bulbs in the same container and these heralds of spring will flower before the lovely leaves re-emerge in late spring.

Garden primroses and polyanthus (*Primula* cultivars) are undemanding plants that flower early in the year. They keep on blooming for weeks, with pretty patterned flowers on individual stems or clusters on one stem above rosettes of textured leaves. The wild species come from habitats throughout the northern hemisphere, from marshlands to woods to mountains, so plant breeders have produced cultivars for a range of aspects, from full sun to deep shade, and lovely ones for a cool spot indoors.

Window boxes and ledges

Window ledges are like mini-balconies. Sun and shade, wind and damp – all the same considerations when you're thinking about what to plant. Only the dimensions are different. This is a chance to really focus on the detail. Use smaller plants that nevertheless pack a punch with jewel-like flowers over long periods. Plant just one cultivar or create patterns with a range of flower shapes and colours. Make a bold statement with a dramatic leaf or structure on repeat. Track the seasons with bulbs for spring and autumn. Experiment with edibles, growing salads and herbs from seed. This is micro-gardening, but with satisfaction on a macro scale.

And in other news, window boxes are the perfect place for fragrant flowers, their scents wafting in on the breeze and billowing through your home.

Brilliant near and far – the pelargonium is the king of sunny window boxes

Practical makes perfect

A key consideration is access. Your window boxes should be within easy reach. Ideally, you should be able to detach the containers and carry them to wherever you want to do your planting.

Once you've put your window boxes out, you need to be able to water and feed them easily, pinch out and deadhead, harvest food and bouquets, and replace or bulk up plantings.

Just because the plants are outside doesn't mean you can neglect their watering. With their relatively small dimensions, window boxes tend to dry out quickly. And being so close to the building means they're likely to be in a rain shadow – sheltered by the eaves or in the lea of the prevailing winds. While soil-free compost is light and warms up quickly, it also dries out faster than soil-based media, so be prepared to water that much more often. However, just like your indoor plants, outdoor dwellers can become heartily sick if they sit around in water, so make sure your window boxes drain well.

On the subject of draining well, for the sake of neighbourly cohesion, make sure the excess water from your window boxes doesn't drip straight onto the heads of the people downstairs, nor onto their collection of hardy cacti or other xerophytic plants that need to be kept dry.

'Pelargoniums don't like frost, so I take cuttings in autumn and keep them on a cool frost-free windowsill over winter. Or I buy seeds and grow them in spring – they don't take long to reach flowering size.'

Richard Wilford, gardens designer, Kew

Top right, glorious clash of pink bedding begonia above a cascade
of scarlet tuberous begonia and carmine ivy-leaved pelargonium;
top, daffodils nod elegantly above an under planting of cheerful
pansies; below, cyclamen are perfect for window boxes where you
can fully appreciate their exquisite reflexes flowers and patterned
leaves; opposite, a pretty pink pelargonium on a mellow brick wall

Miniature gardens for all seasons

Follow the unfolding year by changing the displays in your window boxes and on window ledges to suit the season. Sunny aspects give you the greatest range of flowers and foliage to choose from.

Spring Window boxes are perfect for smaller daffodil cultivars such as *Narcissus* 'Tête-à-tête' and species tulips such as scarlet *Tulipa praestans* and *Tulipa fosteriana*. Of course, if you want to make a big statement and your window boxes aren't too exposed to the wind, plant taller cultivars.

Winter Garden violas have been bred from species from rocky hillsides and grassy meadows, as have the larger-flowered garden pansies (*Viola tricolor* var. *hortensis*), and their mountain heritage means they can cope with wind, sun, cold and rain, flowering even in the depths of winter. They do better in cooler regions in summer, so if you get great heat, plant them in partial shade.

Summer Coming from rocky exposed South African hillsides, pelargoniums are some of the best plants for window boxes, even flowering more profusely in drier conditions.

Autumn With their bushy foliage and long-lasting flowers, compact cultivars of Michaelmas daisy (*Aster*) and chrysanthemum (*Chrysanthemum* × *morifolium*) make vibrant displays in late summer and autumn.

All year For year-round texture and foliage colour, hardy succulents such as stonecrops (*Sedum*) and houseleeks (*Sempervivum*) are hard to beat. And because they have evolved in rocky habitats in the mountains, they can take a bit of neglect, needing far less water and feeding than leafier, floriferous plants. These dogged survivors even produce flowers that are loved by butterflies.

Edibles You could give over your window boxes to all things edible. In the sun, the so-called 'everbearing' strawberries (*Fragaria* × *ananassa* cultivars) produce their succulent red fruits from June to October – a feast for the eyes as well as the belly. In winter their corrugated, toothed foliage looks fresh, and their fruits are preceded by pretty white flowers.

Full sun and shelter is also needed for chilli peppers, and you can try a trailing tomato such as 'Tumbler' for its heavy crop of cherry-sized toms. Useful and beautiful!

Lettuce, rocket and other leafy greens such as mizuna from Japan can be grown all year round in a sheltered sunny spot (ideally with shade in the middle of the day).

Opposite, succulents provide fascinating texture and structure all year round; below left, sizzling tulips for spring; below, the rich summer cascade of the tuberous begonia lasts until the first frosts; overleaf, blue aster, for vibrant displays into autumn

Small wonder

You may only get sun early or late in the day - if at all - and this makes your window boxes and ledges excellent places for lovely flowering plants from cool mountains and shady forests.

With partial shade, the range of plants is not quite as broad as for brighter aspects, but you can still create floral displays for every season.

Winter warmers Cyclamen come from rocky well-drained Mediterranean places, growing at the base of trees and shrubs. They have adapted to these dry places by developing a big underground tuber for storing water and food during their dormancy in the hot dry summers.

Some, such as florist's cyclamen (*Cyclamen persicum*) are less hardy and should be grown indoors. As well as their gorgeous dainty flowers with reflexed twisting petals, they produce intricately patterned leaves in autumn or late winter. Plant them where their delicate fragrance can waft in through the open window.

Spring cheer Primroses and polyanthus have bright rosettes of textured foliage and

they flower for weeks in spring. They are hardy and withstand harsh weather, so are a good choice for an exposed cool site.

Summer spectacle Trailing petunias and tuberous begonias flower non-stop through summer into early autumn, especially if you keep on deadheading and feeding them.

Some plants perform beautifully even in full shade.

Spring scents As you start opening your windows to let in the fresh spring air, what could be nicer than the scent of flowers wafting into your rooms? Lily-of-the-valley (*Convallaria majalis*) is a shallow-rooting coloniser of mountain woodlands, so is well suited to growing in containers in shade. It has slender mid-green leaves and many white flowers nodding from a slender stem and producing wonderful scent. Auriculas are also highly fragrant. They are hybrids of two mountain primroses (*Primula auricula* and *Primula hirsuta*), so as well as bringing scent and general cottage garden loveliness to your window ledges, they are frost hardy. They need to be kept fairly dry in winter (in the mountains they'd be dry and insulated under the snow), so the rain shadow on the window ledge is ideal. Don't forget to water them well through the growing season.

Summer sizzler Busy Lizzies (*Impatiens*) produce their colourful flowers over long periods, provided they're well fed, watered and deadheaded. Best of all, their origins in the undergrowth of tropical forests mean they thrive in shade.

Opposite, exquisite auriculas; above left, rich colours and a long flowering season from the busy Lizzy; above right, mounds of pretty primula flowers in Spring.

'I wasn't particularly into plants as a kid, but I've always loved primulas – the whole family. I know they're not fancy, but they're really pretty – nice simple flowers, great scent, and so many different colours. And they're really easy to grow. I always have them in a container with reticulate irises. They give you a sense of waking up for spring.'

Kit Strange, bulb specialist, Kew

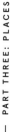

Equally great indoors

Now that we tend to live in double-glazed, sealed buildings for energy efficiency, there isn't such a natural exchange of air between indoors and outdoors. The good news is that plants refresh and clean your air. Really. Just like they do the entire atmosphere.

In the 1980s, in preparation for colonising the Moon (project ongoing), US space agency NASA did a heap of research into creating sustainable life-support systems for migrant earthlings. In the process, they discovered that some plants are really good at cleaning up our environments. Further research in the 1990s demonstrated that as well as refreshing our air by making oxygen, many common houseplants remove the toxins emitted by mass-produced clothes, furniture, wall and floor coverings. And they take out bioeffluents, mould spores and bacteria while they're at it. Studies show that houseplants also raise indoor humidity to healthy levels, countering the dry air created by central heating systems that irritates our noses and throats.

Tilting at windowsills

———

What are windowsills for exactly, if not for
growing plants? If you put your books on them,
they'll fade in the sun. Ditto photographs. Your gadgets
won't like the changes of temperature and humidity.
And windowsills are a no-no for food.

But plants? Windows are old technology but
they're great for plants. And they have these handy
ledges just right for pots and their saucers, out of
the way of the action but, like living paintings,
very much part of the room.

Windowsills get light, more or less depending
on which way they're facing. They're protected from
frost, but if the heating's turned down they can stay
cool in winter, and they experience a dip in temperature
at night. Windows can be opened and closed to control
air circulation. So if your windows have sills (and
if they don't, position a table or a shelf right under
them instead), don't waste them. Get plants!

Ropes and rosettes: delicate colours and intriguing succulent shapes of echeveria, aeonium
and trailing burro's tail; previous page, Clockwise from left: fittonia cuttings sealed in a glass jar,
pitcher plant, rattlesnake plant, the large arrow-shaped leaves of tropical climber *Philodendron*,
bird's nest fern, variegated tufted airplant, and mother-in-law's tongue

Fifty shades of shade

Here's a plant, a houseplant. And here's a windowsill.
Bring them together, *et voila!*

But of course it's not quite that simple. Many houseplants come from the understorey of tropical and subtropical forests. They haven't evolved to cope with frost, and an indoor windowsill will give them the protection they need. But nor have they evolved to deal with direct sunlight. So a windowsill that faces south and receives belting sun all day long won't be ideal.

Equally, a cactus species with spines and hairs, supremely adapted to the extremely high light levels of its desert environment, will struggle on a north-facing window in the weak solar radiation of the northern hemisphere winter.

An east-facing window will get all the brightness of the morning sun but, as the Earth turns, not the intensity and heat of the ripening day, so suits plants from forest margins, such as the leafy dumb cane (see picture on page 186).

The Goldilocks test Some of your rooms will be warmer than others. Humidity will rise and fall too. Your kitchen is likely to be the warmest place and relatively humid, while your living room has temperature swings depending on the life of the household. Bedrooms tend to be cooler and more stable. Bathrooms get steamy but can be cold either side of shower time. Halls and stairwells should be less heated and, if they lead to the outside world, might be draughty.

For your indoor plants, some windowsills will be too hot, some too cold and some just right. Just like Goldilocks's porridge.

Other chapters deal with plants for specific rooms, but on these pages you'll find some ideas for making the most of windowsills whatever their location in the house.

Left, Arabian jasmine arches its flower buds over a stocky cactus, slender *Aloe vera* and the toothed mounding foliage of *Aloe brevifolia*; opposite, a spiky slender airplant

Sunny windowsill

There aren't very many plants that are robust enough
to survive on a windowsill that gets sun all day long
in summer. But the cacti species that come from exposed
arid places have evolved to survive the searing heat
and fierce light of the desert in summer.

THE FIBONACCI SERIES

Many of the patterns of the natural world – repeats and spirals and syncopation – can be described using mathematical formulas. An Italian called Fibonacci introduced one of these formulas to Europe in 1202 (although it had been part of Indian mathematics for at least 600 years before that). The Fibonacci series describes spirals that are fractals – shapes that can be split into parts, each of which is a smaller copy of the whole. They can be found in the branching of trees, the arrangement of leaves on stems, the seedheads of sunflowers, and the bracts of a pinecone. In fact, they're everywhere you look – in snail shells and galaxies and human fingerprints.

The cactus' network of spines and their often hairy or woolly covering act as sunscreens. Their habitats tend to have low humidity too, so cacti are able to deal with the dry air caused by central heating. So while a very humid bathroom isn't ideal for cacti, in general you'll find they thrive pretty much anywhere indoors in the sun.

Like cacti, living stones (*Lithops*), moonstones (*Pachyphytum oviferum*) and echeveria come from semi-deserts and will grow in full light anywhere in the house.

Although bougainvilleas (*Bougainvillea × buttiana*) originate from rocky hillsides of South America, they are vigorous climbers that aim for the sun. If you get frosts in your area, grow this plant in full sun on an indoor windowsill and you'll be rewarded with large clusters of brilliant blooms from summer to autumn. In late winter or early spring, prune it to keep it in check, cutting the side shoots back to within three or four buds of the woody framework. See picture on page 125.

Sun-loving succulents; cacti (opposite), echeverias and sedums (above) and lithops (right)

Bright windowsill, no direct sun

Few plants really thrive if they get full sun all summer long - even the cacti and succulents appreciate a bit of protection at the height of the season - and many grow well in bright light out of reach of the harsher rays from our nearest star.

Most houseplants from the arum family – such as the Swiss cheese plant (*Monstera*) and heart-leaf plant (*Philodendron scandens*) – flower extremely rarely. But flamingo flowers (*Anthurium andraeanum* and *Anthurium scherzerianum*) and peace lilies (*Spathiphyllum wallisii*) produce long-lasting flowers with dramatic 'hoods' (called spathes) throughout the year. In spite of their origins in moist tropical forests of South and Central America, they tolerate a drier atmosphere. But to keep them in tip-top condition, raise the humidity around their foliage by standing their pots on a saucer of wet gravel.

Haworthias are perennial succulents related to the aloe (see *Structural* on page 109). They come from the lowlands of southern Africa and are treasured as houseplants for their well-defined fleshy structures, often patterned with bright tubercles, or nodules. Some of them have a fascinating adaptation called a leaf or epidermal window. This is a translucent part of the leaf, usually at its apex, that allows sunlight to enter its interior. So even if most of the plant remains below the surface of the soil, where it is protected from extreme heat and drying winds, nevertheless photosynthesis can take place, because radiant energy can enter the leaf. Living stones (*Lithops*) also have this adaptation. Indoors, haworthias don't need to retreat underground as the environment is (hopefully) less harsh. In winter, low light and low temperatures send haworthias into dormancy, so they should be kept dry.

The winter garden The windowsill of a cool bright hall that doesn't get damp is good for overwintering petunia cuttings and cut-back pelargoniums and fuchsias, and for starting off tomatoes and lettuces from seed. It's also handy for inducing dormancy in plants such as cacti and tender succulents, allowing them to tick over quietly until light levels stimulate them back into growth. You can gradually increase watering as their metabolism revives, preparing them for outside conditions or a return to their warm sunny windowsills in summer.

'I grow succulents and cacti in a shallow glazed clay saucer, about 40 cm (15 in) across. Friends call it 'the desert.' If something gets too big, I take it out, propagate it and start again. Just like a big garden, it's an ongoing experiment. It's always evolving. Minimal care and maximum enjoyment.'

Tom Freeth, alpine plants specialist, Kew

Some haworthias (opposite) pull themselves down into the soil to escape the harsh sun of their dryland habitat; above, start your veggie seedlings on a bright windowsill; above right, the elegant silhouettes of a moth orchid and a flamingo flower

Macramé central

There's always a shelf or two in the house that's too high for daily use but great for storing stuff you only need once in a blue moon (Twister, fondue set, one-man tent) or for things too precious to use but that you like to see (the soup tureen you picked up at a flea market, the oversized snow dome with a model of the Empire State Building inside).

There's also always a mysterious hook in the ceiling, left by a previous tenant, or a curtain rail made redundant by blinds.

These are great opportunities to grow climbing and cascading plants from the tropics and subtropics. Many of them grow enormous in their natural habitats – scaling a large rainforest tree, even partially, requires impressive dimensions – but in general the domestic environment curtails their wild vigour. And if not, you just have to get good at pruning.

For plants to hang in humid bathrooms, see *Bathroom* on page 187.

Mistletoe cactus comes from rainforests where it grows on trees and damp rocks (see page 188)

Masters of suspense

—

Many plants have adapted to grow on other plants in their
natural habitats, hitching a ride towards light and water
or escaping the dangers of grazing animals.

Unlike in the forest, where the sun is overhead, the light in our homes tends to come from the side, so you can persuade your climbing plants to grow laterally rather than straight up.

A high shelf gives a plant space to stretch its limbs. And you get to appreciate the angles, swags and tendrils, and coax them into displaying their foliage (and flowers) to best effect. Likewise, hanging their containers brings plants up to eye level or higher, so you can really appreciate the detail. They decorate your wall like living 3D paintings or bring depth and interest to a redundant corner with their texture and colour.

Sunny spot Star jasmine (*Jasminum polyanthum*) is a twining evergreen climber from China and can grow to 3 m (10 ft) – handy if you want to create a screen to filter the light and keep the temperature down in summer. It flowers in winter and its slender white blooms waft wonderful scent through your living area (see *Social climbers* page 32).

Silvery-grey air plants (*Tillandsia*) love the sun. Their complex leaf surfaces are covered in fine structures made from dead cells filled with air, which act as a wick to draw moisture from their surroundings into their cells. If you soak this plant, water enters these air-filled cells and you can see through them to the green tissue underneath. The rough surfaces also collect dust from the surrounding air, providing the plant with nutrition. Over time, a plant will produce offsets and can develop

into a large colony. Hang air plants outside in high summer to catch rain, but most of the year keep them indoors – tie them to an interesting branch between the leaves. After a while, if the plant is flourishing, it will attach itself to the branch with roots.

You wouldn't expect succulents in *Macramé central*, but two species make fantastic hanging displays. String of beads (*Senecio rowleyanus*) is actually a member of the daisy family but produces – well – strings of beads! It comes from exposed rocky habitats in south-west Africa, producing trailing stems with leaves like plump green peas. This globular shape reduces water loss through evaporation.

Burro's tail (*Sedum morganianum*) is a succulent that sprawls from the rocky cliffs of ravines in Mexico and makes a dramatic subject for a hanging basket, with long dangling stems covered in pale blue-green fleshy leaves (see picture on page 182).

'I wouldn't be without *Senecio rowleyanus* – I live in a flat where all the windows face south, so most houseplants get burnt to a crisp, but this grows really well. It's very structural – perfect green spheres on a string. And you can grow it in unusual containers, even trailing out of a wine glass!

Luke Gunner, student horticulturist, Kew

--- SHARE ALERT ---

Burro's tail is quite brittle, and sections detach at the slightest touch, but each length will root easily in an airy compost to produce new plants.

Opposite, replicate the natural high rise homes of airplant by attaching them to suspended branches; above, string-of-beads (*Senecio rowleyanus*)

'I grow hearts on a string (*Ceropegia linearis* subsp. *woodii*), which is a really unusual succulent from southern Africa. It has thin stems with heart-shaped leaves and it trails over the mantelpiece.'

Nick Woods, seasonal displays, Kew

Bright and breezy Get the leafy vibes of 1970s interior decor with a cascade of spider plants (*Chlorophytum*) and spiderworts (*Tradescantia*). Spider plants come from the undergrowth of forested slopes, flat terrain and on cliffs, growing in large colonies. If you hang them up in their marvellous macramé cradle, they will still try to colonise, throwing out slender arching shoots with tiny spiderettes at their ends, over time creating a mass of spiky satellites around the mother ship. Spiderworts (*Tradescantia zebrina* and *Tradescantia fluminensis*) have lax juicy stems and bulk up in a relatively short time. Their elegant stripy green and white leaves tend to have purple stains around the base and on the underside. They even flower – bright three-petalled blooms throughout the year. They are great for houseplant novices. In their natural habitats, they scramble through open scrub. In the home, they can tolerate a little bit of overwatering, aren't too fussy about humidity or light levels (as long as it's not full sun) and prefer to be a bit cooler than your average Joe from the tropics (see picture on page 184).

Summer evenings indoors take on a tropical vibe with the sweet scent of the wax plant (*Hoya carnosa*). The clusters of star-shaped white to pale pink flowers with their glistening nectar look almost artificial in low light. Though this climber comes from lowland tropical rainforests in India, Burma and China, it doesn't need high temperatures to thrive. Let it sprawl along a shelf or train it over a lattice of bamboo.

GET PLANTS

Above, optimising the window space by hanging trailing pepperomia, leafy alocasia and several orchids above the rest of the plant collection; opposite, the sumptuous leaves of a variegated devil's ivy; far right, maidenhair fern, tiny airplant and spider plant

During the day, the scent of the white waxy flowers of bridal wreath (*Stephanotis floribunda*) takes over from the wax plant. Another evergreen climber, this time from tropical forests in Madagascar, it needs a slightly warmer spot and regular pruning and training throughout the year to keep it from spiralling through your rooms.

High life, low light For shady, sinuous drama, grow tropical climbers from the arum family. These beautiful foliage plants rarely flower, but their glossy foliage brings light and structure to darker rooms.

Devil's ivy (*Epipremnum aureum*) – sometimes known as golden pothos – is a very exuberant climber in its native forests of the South Pacific islands, but is a bit more restrained as a houseplant, growing up to 3 m (10 ft). Train it up a moss pole to create a pillar of glossy yellow-marbled leaves or allow it to tumble from a shelf or hanging pot. The more shade you give it, the less variegation will be displayed in the foliage. It can be pruned throughout the year to keep it from grabbing you as you pass. The heart-leaf plant (*Philodendron scandens*) has even bigger, and just as shiny, deep-green heart-shaped leaves and can grow up to 3 m (10 ft) indoors. Allow it to trail from a pot or train it to twine up a column. Its botanical name, *Philodendron*, comes from the Greek words *phileo*, meaning love, and *dendron*, meaning tree. Your very own love tree!

Classic cool green elegance comes from the Boston fern (*Nephrolepis exaltata* 'Bostoniensis'), whose mass of arching fronds – which can reach more than 1 m (3 ft) long – make it a brilliant subject for a hanging container. It is derived from a widely occurring species from Florida, Central America, the Caribbean islands and Africa. Despite its tropical origins, it tolerates cool rooms, but enjoys humid conditions (see picture on page 51).

KEW TIP

Avoid misting a Boston fern, as that can encourage fungal disease. Instead, to stop its fronds from going crispy, double pot it, putting the main container inside a slightly larger one lined with sphagnum moss (or any hanging basket liner). Keep this layer damp and the moisture will evaporate into the fronds above, creating a lovely humid microclimate.

Stairwell to heaven

So you're rushing out of the building – on your way
to work or meeting friends or whatever – and as you leap
down the stairs past a blur of green you think to yourself:
'I must remember to water that plant!' A few days
later, you're rushing out of the house, on your way
to work or meeting friends, etc, etc, and as you leap
down the stairs past a blur of green you are hit by a sense
of *déjà vu*. Hah. You forgot, didn't you? Forgot to water
that marvellous plant. That's the thing about stairwells.
Generally, you're passing through, with some kind
of deadline. You're distracted and you haven't got
time to run back upstairs and get the watering can.
Clearly, for a stairwell you need plants that can
tolerate a serious amount of neglect.

The plants on these pages deserve your admiration.
Not only are they handsome. Not only do they grow to
fairly substantial sizes and bring structure and natural
beauty to your stairwell. But they are stoic like the Stoics.
They tolerate a range of light conditions (apart from
full-on blazing sunshine throughout the day). They put
up with drought, draughts, dust, low temperatures,
root congestion and lightning. (Wait a minute,
that last one was a joke. Not lightning.
Don't even think about it!)

Robust and beautiful; mother-in-law's tongue

Graceful sentries

A stairwell can be dead space. Let plants bring it to life.

Cool stairwell, bright light If there's too much competition, you move sideways (metaphorically speaking). You evolve to exploit an environmental niche where there's less competition. Or you find strategies to outcompete the neighbours. There's an advantage to being able to survive long periods without water in a region that has a dry season or in a forest that has such a dense canopy that the rain rarely penetrates to the ground.

Make a statement on the stairs with a mother-in-law's tongue (*Sansevieria trifasciata*). In their natural habitat they form colonies of erect, dramatically patterned sword-shaped leaves that can be more than 1.5 m (5 ft) tall. They come from arid rocky places in tropical West Africa, so they tolerate dry air. You feminists will of course eschew its common name of mother-in-law's tongue, but luckily it also goes by the name of snake plant, so you may prefer to use this when trying to track down one of these fabulous plants (see picture on page 176).

Aspidistra (*Aspidistra elatior*) is a real trooper, surviving all manner of neglect. It was a favourite of the 19th-century middle classes, bringing lush greenness to cavernous dark halls. It needs a slightly warmer space than the mother-in-law's tongue.

Bright and warm Of all the palms, the parlour palm (*Chamaedorea elegans*) is the most versatile, as far as positioning goes. Coming from the understorey of Central American woodlands, it tolerates quite a bit of shade, moderate temperatures and moderate humidity. Bright light will encourage this elegant fast-growing plant, which can reach 2 m (6 ft) or more in good conditions, cutting a fine figure on the stairs.

Sunny stairwell The magnificently weird elephant's foot or ponytail palm (*Beaucarnea recurvata*) comes from scrubby semi-deserts in Mexico, where it grows into an impressive tree of more than 4 m (13 ft), and is adapted to full sun, dry air and drought. So it needs a sunny position, but also tolerates fairly cool temperatures – down to about 7°C (45°F). While it can cope with neglect, for best performance it does need a thorough watering a few times a month. Even as a relatively young plant, its thick stem and top knots of strappy curling leaves make it a striking companion, but it can grow up to 1.8 m (6 ft) tall and takes on an imposing architectural character that can't be ignored. It may be some time between buzzing your visitors in downstairs and their arrival at your front door, as they loiter on the stairs getting to know this wonderful cartoon-like creature.

Another dramatic character from Central America is the spineless yucca (*Yucca gigantea*, often labelled *Yucca elephantipes*). Like the elephant's foot, it has adapted to drought by developing a thick trunk that stores water, and it can grow into a big tree of 9 m (30 ft). Even as a houseplant this fine creature grows up to 2.5 m (8 ft) tall, so it needs a bit of space. However, unlike some of its cousins, its long leathery leaves have soft edges and tips, so they're not going to ambush you or your visitors as you go past. They will merely salute you and you will be delighted.

Opposite, the versatile parlour palm brings elegance to the stairwell while above, elephant's foot or ponytail palm injects a touch of weird (seen here with a mighty jade plant); top left, aspidistra survives all manner of neglect and still looks handsome

All about the hall

———

Entrance halls can be chaotic places. Especially
in winter – coats and jackets, boots and umbrellas,
rucksacks and panniers. Year round, it's the place where
sports kits and bikes are stashed. But if your entrance
hall gets natural light, it's worth making space
for a plant, to bring a bit of calm to that transitory
space or to brighten up and beautify the entrance
to your private world.

Hall plants need to be robust and in very stable
containers – otherwise they'll be knocked over
or damaged by passing humans – or pets. If there's
a dog in your home, the hall is the stage for great
displays of excitement when a w.a.l.k. appears
to be on the cards or visitors arrive.

If your hall opens directly onto the great outdoors,
it will be subject to ups and downs, sometimes quite
extreme – blasts of summer heat or cold wind in the
depths of winter. So it's not the place for tropical forest
plants that enjoy a fairly constant temperature and
humidity. But as it's not usually overheated, it's a great
place for plants that like an airy environment. And it's
a very useful refuge for overwintering plants.

Opposite, Kentia palm, rattlesnake plant and peacock plant
need a bright hall that isn't too draughty

Airy fairy or stable shelter?

If there's a buffer between your hall and the outside world then you can introduce plants that prefer a more stable environment.

'I love scented pelargoniums. They were one of the collections I was responsible for in the first glasshouse I worked in. Grow them in the porch and every time you walk through your door you'll get that amazing fragrance.'

Joe Archer, kitchen gardener, Kew

A sunny porch that gets regular blasts of fresh air from your comings and goings is ideal for tender plants that need protection from frost. As they originate in more arid environments where there can be a big difference between daytime and night-time temperatures.

It's also a good spot for overwintering cuttings of sun-loving plants and autumn-sown seedlings, so they're in tip-top condition for planting out when conditions are right.

Brash summer florals such as garden pelargoniums, whose parent species come from dry rocky hillsides in south-western South Africa, will thrive in a sunny, draughty place. Track down species with scented foliage (from peppermint and citrus to eucalyptus and nutmeg) for an extra special welcome.

For year-round structure, cacti from arid habitats are adapted to deal with bright sunshine and high daytime temperatures – in fact they need sun in order to flower. Many species are adapted for low temperatures at night too – some of them are even frost hardy. But the porch provides shelter from the main

threat of cooler climates – too much water in the form of rain. Keep your spiny cacti on a raised shelf where they won't snag you as you pass – columnar types such as *Oreocereus* or *Trichocereus* are best for confined spaces!

Colourful rosette plants such as echeverias and aeoniums hail from arid habitats and, like cacti, will appreciate shelter from too much rain. They will love the raised summer temperatures of an enclosed space but enjoy the low humidity that comes with lots of fresh air.

'As well as the crazy floral kalanchoe cultivars, there are some lovely species. I grow the feltbush (*Kalanchoe beharensis*) from Madagascar. The leaves have a velvety texture and are arrow shaped and undulating, so the whole plant is an interesting shape. They are pale olive but covered in brown hairs, which gives them their softness.'

Lara Jewitt, tender and tropical plant specialist, Kew

Opposite, the unusual trailing succulent, burro's tail; above left, cacti and pitcher plants can tolerate full sun; above, the crazy floral Flaming Katy *Kalanchoe*

‘Haworthias are very forgiving plants. They thrive on neglect. You just have to watch for when the leaves start to wrinkle – that tells you they need watering.’

Sue Skinner, alpine specialist, Kew

Haworthias are perfect for a ledge or shelf in indirect bright light, raised up so you can appreciate their strange forms as you go by. Unusually for succulents, they are better off without full sun and their hard-edged rosettes soon bulk up, forming colonies of offsets.

Because they come from the understorey and margins of tropical forests in the Americas, peacock plants and rattlesnake plants (*Calathea makoyana* and *Calathea lancifolia*) need high humidity and protection from draughts. But they aren't total divas – they will take a certain amount of shade, something that seems to enhance their beautifully patterned leaf markings, and they are perfect for a big warm hall. Water them freely in the growing season and moderately in winter.

As befits their lax trailing foliage, spiderworts (*Tradescantia*) are more laid back than those large-leaved lovelies. They tolerate temperatures as low as 10°C (50°F) and because

they're from open scrubland, they don't need high humidity. A wide shelf or windowsill in bright filtered light will allow them to cascade their stripy purple-stained limbs. The sumptuous leaves of elephant's ear point to its origins in tropical and subtropical forests. It needs bright light and a draught-free warm place and will reward you with exotic drama (pictured opposite and on page 204).

Life in the woodlands of the Himalayas has prepared the aspidistra (*Aspidistra*) for deep shade, swings in temperature and neglect. And still it produces its statuesque pointed leaves, making it the classic plant of the dark elegant hallway. Variegated cultivars add tonal structure to this handsome long-lived yet underrated performer (see picture on page 179).

Opposite, elephant ear; above left, rattlesnake plant, peacock plant and spiderwort; above, haworthias come in many intriguing forms

Bathroom

———

Share the most intimate room in your home
with some plants. They'll need to be able to tolerate
swings in humidity and temperature. Some housemates
like a short sharp shower. Others loiter for hours
in a steamy bath. The air fizzes with chemicals –
deodorant, toothpaste, hairspray, aromatic oils,
shower gel and shampoo, while damp towels and hand
washing keep the humidity high. So, winter or summer,
the windows get thrown open to let in some fresh
air and the temperature plunges.

But if the plants are sheltered from the open
window – hung on the shower rail or positioned
on a shelf in good light (but not direct sun) – many
kinds will thrive. Of course, this is the place for
ferns and foliage plants that grow at ground level
in moist shady tropical and subtropical forests, but also
for the unusual epiphytic cacti, orchids and bromeliads
that have evolved in similar habitats.

Opposite, dumb cane and maidenhair fern catch the light

Hanging baskets for humid spaces

Maximise your bathroom shelf space and mimic the natural habitat of your plants from humid tropical forests by hanging them up.

Epiphytic plants grow not in the soil but on other plants or rocks, using their hosts for support but, unlike parasites, surviving under their own steam by photosynthesising and getting water and nutrients from the atmosphere. The steamy bathroom with bright filtered light can replicate (more or less) the humidity of their natural habitats and they can be suspended in all manner of ingenious ways, so you can pretend you're showering in a waterfall above a *cenote*, or sinkhole, in the middle of a rainforest.

Mistletoe cactus (*Rhipsalis baccifera*) is the most widespread cactus species in the world, growing on trees and damp rocks in moist tropical forests in the Americas and the Caribbean, and even in mangrove swamps in Florida. It is the only true cactus occurring in the Old World and scientists are still speculating about how it spread through Africa and Sri Lanka. It has very slender, acutely branching, pendent stems that can grow 3–4 m (10–13 ft) long, making a really dense grassy curtain. Clusters of small white flowers in winter and early spring are followed by white spherical fruits, which explains the common name.

If the slender pendent ribbed stems of the rat's tail cactus weren't reason enough to grow it, then its striking purple-red flowers borne in spring should clinch it (their shape and colour are classic indicators of hummingbird pollination). The rat's tail cactus (*Disocactus flagelliformis*, sometimes labelled *Aporocactus flagelliformis*) is an epiphyte from open woodlands of Mexico and Central America, trailing over rocks or from the branches of trees, so it needs filtered light and a frost-free sheltered position. It tolerates temperatures down to 7°C (45°F), but hopefully your bathroom won't get that cold. Brrr.

Opposite and right, mistletoe cactus comes from tropical forests and will appreciate a steamy bathroom; below right, spider plant; below left, moth orchids grow on trees in the wild, so make them feel right at home by hanging them up

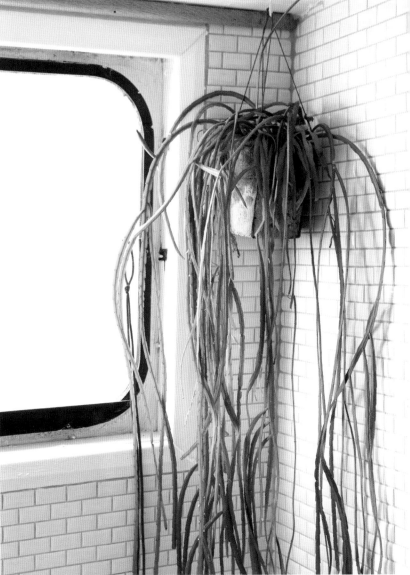

Another epiphyte that needs more warmth than the cacti is the moth orchid (*Phalaenopsis* cultivars), a stunner for the bathroom, with its fleshy leaves and long-lasting waxy large-petalled flowers. The cultivars are derived from species that have adapted to the shade and humidity under the tree canopy of south-east Asian tropical forests (see *Elegant* page 52).

Moving away from the epiphytes, that fabulous retro stalwart the spider plant (*Chlorophytum comosum*) will thrive in the bathroom too (see *Retro* page 103).

Twilight zone

Even bathrooms with low light levels can become sumptuous green retreats with lush fronds and foliage from ferns and plants from the forest floor.

The lovely fronds of the delta maidenhair fern (*Adiantum raddianum*) arc like a waterfall of fresh green droplets. Suitable either for a hanging container or a pot on a shelf – it grows both on rocks and in the ground – it enjoys the humidity that would be found in its natural habitats in the tropical forests of the Americas and the Caribbean islands. It's a good companion for the rat's tail cactus, as it also tolerates fairly low temperatures, down to 7°C (45°F), and needs good ventilation. The trailing maidenhair fern (*Adiantum caudatum*), which comes from the other side of the world in East Asia, makes another fantastic subject for a hanging container, its fronds also reaching 60 cm (2 ft) in length.

The impressive blue star fern (*Polypodium* or *Phlebodium aureum*) is another amazing epiphyte from South American tropical forests (and therefore good for a life of suspense), its arching blue-green edged fronds reaching 75 cm (2.5 ft) long.

Plants from the rainforest floor tend to have large lustrous leaves, so they can gather what little light makes it through the dense tree canopy. Dumb cane (*Dieffenbachia seguine*, sometimes labelled *Dieffenbachia maculata*) comes from rainforests in Brazil and has large green fleshy leaves with strong creamy-white or yellow patterns in spots or splashes. Give it a bright position in the bathroom, out of direct sun, only watering it when dry.

The markings on the dumb cane's leaves are known as variegation – and variegated leaves occur when patches of cells don't produce the green pigment chlorophyll. Markings are often less dramatic in deep shade, as the plant needs to work harder to manufacture sugars through photosynthesis, and it can only do that in the cells where chlorophyll is present. So if you want your variegated plant to keep its patterns sharp, stand it in bright but indirect light.

Other big-leaved plants from the rainforest floor with wonderful leaf markings, such as peacock and rattlesnake plants (*Calathea* – see *Hall* page 180), will respond well to the humidity too, as long as the window isn't being opened on too regular a basis, causing the temperature to swing.

Opposite, the undulating fronds of the blue star fern; left, dumb cane and maidenhair fern come from the forest floor and therefore are tolerant of shade

Kitchen

The kitchen is the heart of the home. Light, bright and busy. After all, everyone needs to eat. If there are cooks in your household, your kitchen is likely to get quite warm. The water boiled by avid tea and coffee drinkers will raise the humidity too. (Respect to tea and coffee plants, by the way, which originate in the mountains of Asia and Africa and have conquered the world!)

Even if ready meals and take-aways are more often on the menu, the kitchen is likely to experience big swings in temperature and humidity – windows being opened after burnt toast in the morning and late at night, people coming and going, steam from hot food and drinks (not to mention hot air from politicians on the radio), the heat from the back of the refrigerator and damp from the latest basket full of laundry waiting to be hung up to dry.

As you're often in there – preparing food, eating and chatting – you'll see your plants every day. That way you'll get to know them and become attuned to their needs. (Water alert: just because you see them every day, doesn't mean you need to water them every day. Overwatering is the main killer of houseplants.)

Clockwise from top right; vanda orchid with Spanish moss trailing from the same pot, an actual pineapple, flower spike and stiff rounded leaves of moth orchid cultivar 'Panda', the tall slender leaf of *Amorphophallus* 'Konjac', and a colony of spiky air plants

Herbs to hand

The airy, sunny windowsill is the Spanish hillside or the open steppe. In the kitchen, it's the place for plants you can cook with. So which plants work in this hub of your home? Well, if there's no natural light at all, then sorry, the kitchen is no place for a plant. But more often than not the kitchen offers a choice of growing places.

Most of our culinary herbs are from Mediterranean climates with strong sunlight and hot dry summers (see *Natural* page 70). Your sunny, airy windowsill – where the window is often thrown open in summer to keep the air moving – is an ideal spot for vitamin-rich leafy herbs and spice plants that pack a punch. It's a veritable throne for the king of Italian cuisine, basil (*Ocimum basilicum*), and the queen of the eastern palate, coriander or, in the US, cilantro (*Coriandrum sativum*). Grow them from seed and harvest leaves as required. Just what a kitchen needs – evocative aromas and zingy green freshness. As for the knave of the ancient Americas, the chilli pepper (*Capsicum*), what could give you a finer display than those shiny vibrant fruits, promising culinary explosions?

If you're lucky enough to have outside space for your herbs and chillies, your sunny airy windowsill is a great place for cacti and succulents, which need low humidity and high light levels (apart from the rainforest cacti – see *Bathroom* on page 188). Team up some squat woolly cacti with the jagged fleshy blue-green spikes of *Aloe vera* to throw interesting shadows into the room.

Winter refuge In winter, the sunny kitchen windowsill is a warm, bright refuge for pots of herbs – especially in parts of the world that experience sub-zero temperatures for weeks on end, conditions that rosemary, thyme and sage struggle to survive. Even in the darkest months, these plants of rocky

sun-soaked hillsides yield fragrant sprigs for food and teas. Water them sparingly until they start to shoot in spring, preparing themselves for summer *al fresco* in the yard or on the balcony.

'The plant I couldn't be without is *Aloe vera*. I love the summer and the sun, and having this plant in my home always reminds me of it (plus it's the best product to use for the occasional sunburn). I enjoy growing plants that not only look good but can also be used in other ways.'

Rebecca Hilgenhof, tender plants specialist, Kew

Supermarkets offer beautiful-looking pots of leafy herbs, but they are rammed with lots of small individual plants all squashed in together and aren't meant to last. When you get them home, take them out of the pot, split the rootball into four or five clumps and repot into fresh compost. With sunshine, careful watering and a weekly liquid feed, you'll be harvesting for months instead of days. Plus, you can share extras among your friends.

Sun lovers: opposite, chilli pepper, Moroccan mint and basil; above right, the fleshy spikes of *Aloe vera*; above left, squat plump cacti

Counter intuitive

Kitchen surfaces see a lot of action so it's important that your potted plants are robust and portable. They mustn't object to being moved around to accommodate guests, large-scale culinary or other creative projects, or regular unpacking and sorting of foodstuffs brought back by hunter-gatherers returning from the big wide world.

Bright spot If your kitchen is a calm oasis, the African violet and Cape primrose (*Saintpaulia ionautha, Streptocarpus rexii* cultivars – see *Charming* page 96) are hard to beat for compact charm and colour. Reproduce the shady moist environment of their rocky natural habitat by keeping them out of direct sun but somewhere bright near the washing-up bowl and the hob, where they will thrive in the raised humidity.

If you have a little more space, add some tropical drama to the kitchen with the long-lasting blooms and glossy leaves of peace lilies (*Spathiphyllum*) and flamingo flowers (*Anthurium*) (see *Dramatic* page 25), or the brilliant flower and foliage spikes of the forest bromeliads (see flaming sword, pictured opposite).

Slow-growing jade plant (*Crassula ovata*) brings robust succulent structure to the kitchen. Out of direct sunlight, the fleshy leaves stay deep green and the branching stems make it look like a small tree. Its small white starry flowers are produced in autumn.

Easter cactus (*Hatiora gaertneri*) is one of the forest cacti, enjoying bright light and humidity, producing brilliant trumpet-shaped flowers from flattened, segmented stems.

Shady shelf From the mountain forests of northern India comes the king or painted-leaf begonia (*Begonia rex*), from which plant breeders have created some spectacular foliage plants. A shelf at eye level will allow you to appreciate the entrancing metallic sheen of many cultivars, which seems to be enhanced by low light. If the air is too dry, the margins

of these beautifully textured leaves can become crispy, so the tea-drinker's kitchen is the place to be.

'The coconut palm (*Cocos nucifera*) is easy to grow in a bright humid place in your kitchen or bathroom. The young plants are really architectural and I like the fact that coconuts have a hundred and one uses.'

David Cooke, temperate plants specialist, Kew

'Don't throw away your coffee grounds or tea leaves – instead, add them to your compost bin to improve your soil structure and fertilise at the same time. Be aware that both need to be rinsed beforehand as they can alter the pH – making it more acid – which some plants may not like!'

Rebecca Hilgenhof, tender plants specialist, Kew

Opposite, jade plants; above right, flaming sword bromeliad; top, Easter cactus; below, the painted leaves of the rex or king begonia

Living room

Usually the largest room in the house, the living room also has to be the most versatile. Chill-out zone, gaming hotspot, study space, fitness studio, cinema, party room. The living room can accommodate a big show-off that fills a corner with interest, a platoon of spiky characters standing to attention on the sideboard, glossy foliage tumbling from a high shelf and smaller curiosities for the coffee table, to contemplate on a lazy Sunday morning.

The living room is usually well served with natural light and kept at a comfortable temperature for sedentary humans, without big swings in temperature or cold draughts. And what's nice for people suits a good range of houseplants too – even those from tropical rainforests, surprisingly.

In the summer humidity can be high, but in the winter central heating can dry out the atmosphere – so in spite of the warmth, the environment might not suit plants from tropical and subtropical forests. To raise the humidity around your plant, place its pot in a pebble tray – a deep saucer containing a layer of stones – filled with water to just below the surface of the stones. The water will steadily evaporate (so it needs topping up), creating a microclimate around the plant.

Handsome specimens: bottle palm and fiddle leaf fig

Lounging around

If your living room gets a lot of direct sunshine, some of your plants might become uncomfortable, even though they're from the tropics.

Your living room might be big enough for some graceful palms, but most of them come from forests, and aren't too happy in full sun. However the lovely sentry or Kentia palm (*Howea forsteriana*) comes from a tiny island in the Tasman Sea, 600 km (370 miles) north east of Sydney, Australia. Lord Howe Island has a subtropical climate and stays cool in summer (26°C/79°F maximum) thanks to the sea breezes. So, as the dominant tree species on the island, the Kentia palm is adapted to relatively dry air and can deal with central heating, even when grown in full sun. Plus the optimum room temperature for humans is just right for it. While the elegant spreading leaves of this slender-stemmed lovely can reach 2–3 m (6–10 ft) in length, it's a slow developer, so is unlikely to outgrow its welcome too soon (see picture on page 180).

The Chinese rose (*Hibiscus rosa-sinensis*), with its shiny deep green leaves, dense bushiness and silky trumpet flowers, sometimes with ruffled or pleated petals, makes the perfect houseplant. In fact it has been in cultivation for so long that no one is entirely sure of its natural origins. It's likely that it comes from tropical Asia, and it thrives in a warm sunny position where the temperature doesn't fluctuate too much. There are some lovely *Hibiscus* cultivars that are hardy enough to grow outside, even in areas with fairly severe winters (see *Elegant* page 55).

Big and bold: left to right, elephant's foot or ponytail palm, jade plant, bottle palm, fiddle leaf fig; opposite, show-stopping hippeastrum; pitcher plant in the late afternoon sun; overleaf, their colours may be muted, but an assembly of succulents makes a striking display

The outrageous trumpet-shaped flowers of the hippeastrum, or amaryllis (*Hippeastrum*), produced in the depths of winter, can't fail to stop you in your tracks. Bred from equally show-stopping species, mostly from rocky habitats and stream banks in Brazil, it doesn't need high humidity. Just give it sun and warmth – along with lots of water when it comes into growth – and it will reward you with a stunning display.

The dry air that comes from central heating won't bother cacti from arid regions, but sunshine or at least very bright light is a must.

En masse, succulents form a highly ornamental assembly of muted khaki, green and marine-hued structures - and their origins in the dry lands of the American and African continents mean they're suited to low humidity that comes with central heating (see picture overleaf).

Leafy lustre

Out of reach of the harsh rays of the summer sun, plants from tropical forests have enough character to be your flatmates (only don't ask them to pay the rent).

For sumptuous texture and striking patterns, grow elephant's ear (*Alocasia* cultivars) in a bright warm corner sheltered from draughts, where the humidity will be higher. Its parent species grow in streamsides and marshes in the tropics of south-east Asia and it needs regular watering. Raise the humidity by standing its pot in a pebble tray – a deep saucer containing a layer of gravel and water that will evaporate into the foliage above.

Retro drama comes from the large leaves and sinuous stems of the Swiss cheese plant (*Monstera deliciosa*). Its tropical rainforest origins mean it thrives in the same conditions as the elephant's ear. In fact, if you have the space, grow them together, so they can create a humid microclimate of their own!

Bring architectural light and shade to the living room with species from the forests of tropical Africa – the dragon tree (*Dracaena marginata*) or the areca palm (*Dypsis lutescens*). Give them moderate to bright light, but protection from summer sun. They will tolerate fairy cool temperatures and don't need especially high humidity (see picture on page 206).

Sideboard sophisticates If you can't hang them up (see *Dramatic* on page 33), let the twining evergreen climbers from tropical forests sprawl elegantly over a large surface or train them onto lattices or hoops, so their leafy silhouettes can be admired against the wall. Devil's ivy (*Epipremnum aureum*) lights up darker spaces by reflecting light from its shiny marbled leaves, while bridal wreath (*Stephanotis floribunda*), star jasmine (*Jasminum polyanthum*) and wax plant (*Hoya carnosa*) offer more delicate foliage and highly scented flowers.

Coffee table curiosity A bright side-table is the place where curious beauty and detail can be appreciated close up. Entrance your visitors with strange air plants (*Tillandsia*), whose scaly foliage takes on a velvety sheen. Whether you display them on weathered wood or glittering glass, their audacious disregard for our conventional idea of plants – growing in the ground, for example – is striking. Their tiny scales help them harvest water and nutritious dust from the air around them, particularly

from mists and low cloud. Hopefully, you won't have any such weather phenomena in your living room, but while they continue to tick over enigmatically in dry conditions, they will need a thorough drenching – preferably with rainwater – from time to time. Make sure they are portable, so you can give them a bath or hang them out in the summer rain (see *Odd* page 86).

Air plants are members of the bromeliad family, and their relatives are among the showiest indoor plants around, some of them with beautifully patterned leaves in addition to the brilliant bracts surrounding their long-lasting flowers. Urn plants (*Aechmea fasciata*), flaming swords (*Vriesea splendens*) and tufted air plants (*Guzmania lingulata*) are plants from tropical forests, so a table that gets good or moderate amounts of natural light, out of draughts, will let you appreciate them up close. You'll also be able to monitor the water levels in the 'cups' formed by their rosettes and keep them topped up with rainwater.

Charismatic companions: opposite, elephant's ear and above left, Swiss cheese plant; above right, urn plant, one of the forest bromeliads; overleaf, the dragon tree and areca palm; overleaf, the magnificent rubber fig commands a stable warm environment in a corner of your living room, out of direct sunlight

Bedroom

———

You spend about a third of your life sleeping. You probably spend rather longer than that in your bedroom. So it's important that you're comfortable. Plants can make a big contribution not only to how your bedroom looks, but also to how it feels.

Central heating desiccates the air and that can irritate your nose and throat. By quietly carrying on with their metabolic processes, bedroom plants help to maintain moderate humidity all year round, keeping your nasal membranes healthy and hydrated in the process.

Studies say that the quality of your sleep has a lot to do with the temperature of your room – a cooler body temperature promoting more deep sleep. So while your living spaces are ideally 18–20°C (64–68°F), which is warm enough for the most tropical of plants, bedrooms should be markedly cooler at 14–16°C (57–61°F), which is suitable for plants that prefer moderate conditions.

Opposite, a cluster of cacti set a subtle, sophisticated tone

Pyjama party

You might want to keep your bedroom serenely green or go for splashes of seasonal colour by introducing flowering plants. Either way, so the scientists say, indoor plants help to create healthy living spaces.

Flowering plants in your bedroom. What could be nicer? And in winter, with fragrance? Perfect! The dainty precise blooms of florist's cyclamen (*Cyclamen persicum*) are produced from early winter to early spring, above their silver-patterned leaves. They come from rocky hillsides in the Mediterranean and North Africa, flowering in the cool winter and retreating underground for the scorching summer, so they will be comfortable on a bright windowsill, their sweet scent as delicate as their twisting petals.

Even when they're not in bloom, flamingo flower hybrids (*Anthurium*) and peace lilies (*Spathiphyllum*) are lovely plants to have in a bright spot out of direct sun. But they are prized for their flowers – being two of the few arum family members to bloom regularly in cultivation – and their flower spikes have elegant cowls that persist for weeks. Although they come from moist tropical forests of South and Central America, they tolerate a drier atmosphere and cool temperatures, down to 15°C (59°F).

Desert cacti, air plants and other succulents need a sunny windowsill. Succulents like jade plant and flaming Katy need their beauty sleep. Jade plants get ten to twelve hours of darkness and cooler temperatures in winter time in Southern Africa, so a sleepyhead whose lie-ins reproduce these conditions is likely to be rewarded with a mass of starry lightly scented flowers in the darkest days of the year. Flaming Katy is also more inclined to flower again given a sustained rest in autumn in a darker cooler place. Another reason to stay in bed!

For early summer flowers and fragrance, there are some lovely miniature roses. They need a spot on a south-facing windowsill in spring, so they can harvest as much sunlight as possible. Throw open the window regularly as they appreciate good air circulation. Once they've flowered, put them outside on a window ledge or in the yard – but don't forget to continue to water and feed them until the weather gets really cold. Then bring them indoors to a cool place to prevent their roots from freezing, and reduce watering dramatically, allowing them a dormant period. In late winter, repot them, bring them back to the bedroom, start watering and watch those beautiful flowers bud up and open.

'The plant I wouldn't be without is *Anthurium clarinervium*, from Mexico. Its leaves are a beautiful shape, with a reticulated vein structure and a kind of iridescence. Its flowers are plain and brown, as if it has expended all its energy on producing its leaves.'

Joanna Bates, seasonal displays specialist, Kew

Opposite (left to right), a wavy-edged hart's tongue fern, the cowled flowers and elegant foliage of the peace lily, brilliant blossoms of flaming Katy, the purple-backed foliage of tradescantia all grow well in bright light out of reach of strong summer sunlight; above, *Cyclamen Persiciem*

Sleeping patterns

Cooler bedrooms can be good places for forest plants, which prefer a slightly more humid atmosphere.

Coming from shady rocky habitats in Tanzania, the African violet (*Saintpaulia ionantha* cultivars), with its pretty flowers and rounded furry deep green leaves, will bring colour and texture to a shelf or table top out of direct sun. Raise the humidity around the plant by sitting it on a pebble tray, regularly topped up with water to just below the surface of the stones.

The top of the wardrobe is a great stage for displaying the cascading foliage of spider plants (*Chlorophytum comosum*) and spiderworts (*Tradescantia*) – see *Macramé central* page 174.

Some shade-loving forest cacti are good for bedrooms, tolerating cooler temperatures down to 10°C (50°F) and moderate humidity. The Christmas cactus (*Schlumbergera truncata* hybrids) and Easter cactus (*Hatiora gaertneri*, formerly known as *Rhipsalidopsis*) grow on tree branches and rocks (as epiphytes) in mountain forests in Brazil. Though their flattened segmented succulent stems look like they've been run over, they arch out of their containers and can make a dramatic display, especially when their brightly coloured funnel-shaped flowers emerge. They look very alike, but the Christmas cactus flowers in late autumn to winter, while the Easter cactus blooms from late spring to midsummer (see picture on page 197).

Some ferns, such as maidenhair fern, will enjoy the cooler less drying conditions of the bedroom, as will the button fern (*Pellaea rotundifolia*). Its native habitat is cliffs and crevices and open forest in New Zealand, so it can be grown in a hanging container or in a pot on a shelf, where its arching fronds will reach 30 cm (1 ft) long.

Year-round rhythmic structure comes from the Zanzibar gem or zeezee plant (*Zamioculcas zamiifolia*), whose fleshy, upright narrow leaves with smooth shiny dark green leaflets emerge directly from a succulent rhizome. However, its succulent character doesn't indicate origins in arid areas – in fact, this tropical East African species comes from rocky habitats in seasonal forests and savannas – but it does have the ability to survive a dry season by becoming dormant. Still, to maintain its evergreen display, water it as soon as its compost feels dry. It can deal with fairly low humidity, cooler temperatures down to 10°C (50°F) and moderate light, growing to 60 cm (2 ft) tall.

Cool customers: above, the delicate fronds of the maidenhair fern; opposite, pretty flowers and luscious leaves of the African violet; top, fine foliage from the king begonia and the strange succulent spikes of zamioculcas.

'Why am I so keen on "foliage begonias"? Just take a look at the leaf shapes, colours and forms. Leaves like multi-coloured inkblots, like marbled paper or jewels or snailshells or funky savoy cabbage leaves. Plants of all sizes, from all kinds of habitats - from moist and shady to perched on limestone cliffs. They flower too - some with the most marvellous scent.'

Sara Redstone, plant health specialist, Kew

PART THREE: PLACES

215

Part Four: Buy, care and share

This section is all about the practical, logistical, technical stuff.

After all, once you've made the decision to get plants, it's easy enough to acquire them. As a general rule, people who are into plants are keen to share them - and then there are the shops! But if you're just starting out, the sheer range of choice is a bit mind boggling. When you've chosen your plant and brought it home, you want to give it the best chance to thrive. But what are its needs? Once you've mastered the art of caring of your plant, you're going to want to share the joy. And, naturally, there are many different ways of doing so.

Here are a few ideas to help you navigate the wonderful world of plant growing.

Buy

If you get your plants from good plant nurseries, they should be healthy and free from disease. It's tempting to buy reduced-price plants from the hospital corner, but until you're a plant ninja with highly developed green fingers, start with plants in the best possible condition. That way you'll know that if something goes wrong, it's likely to be down to your care.

As a general rule, buy plants with lots of unopened buds, and perhaps one or two open flowers so you can see exactly what they look like – then you get to enjoy their peak blooming period when you get them home.

Make sure the leaves look healthy (see *Look after your leaves* on page 228) and check for pests under the leaves and on the buds – the last thing you want to do is to introduce pesky insects or fungal problems to your other botanical friends.

Check the base of the pot – if roots are growing out of the holes, then don't buy the plant. It will already be stressed. Equally, a plant with a feeble root system might not thrive when you get it home.

Goldilocks test: the compost should neither be too wet (except in the case of carnivorous and aquatic plants) nor too dry (except in the case of cacti and succulents).

Provenance

Be sure to buy plants and bulbs from 'cultivated stock'. That way you avoid supporting the trade in wild-collected plants that has devastated some species in their native habitats.

This is really important. Did you know that a third of all cactus species are endangered in the wild? According to the International Union for Conservation of Nature (IUCN), a non-governmental organisation that is the global authority on the status of the natural world, one reason is that habitats are being lost to farming and urban development. But it is also because cacti are being harvested for trade and private collections. Many species occur in very restricted areas – where a particular species grows only in one or two ravines, it is really vulnerable if the developers move in. The situation is just as precarious when plants from small populations are collected from the wild and sold into the plant trade.

There are brilliant plants people out there propagating and growing on from their own stock plants, so there is absolutely no need to collect from the wild just to satisfy our obsessions.

Independent nurseries are often run by people with a great dedication to a particular group of plants – if you're just starting out, or even quite an experienced plant grower yourself, these are the people to seek out for species and cultivars to match your skills and level of interest. Go to your local horticultural shows, make connections, feed your passion.

Care

Compost Let's assume that you are growing your plants in containers. Their **health** depends on the compost, or growing medium, you use. And a growing medium is NOT an enigmatic person in a headscarf who communicates telepathically with dead plants. It is the material you fill your containers with.

You're aiming for a growing medium that can deliver the right amount of **water**, the right balance of **nutrients** and the right **pH** (or level of alkalinity or acidity) for your plants. If you scrunch a handful, it should **crumble** when you open your hand, rather than sticking together. But some plants need more crumbliness than others.

There are two basic types of compost available to buy. Both contain **slow-release fertiliser**. Their contents will have been sterilised to prevent fungal and bacterial problems.

Loam- or **soil-based** compost – based on soil, these also contain organic matter, and grit or sand. Loam-based composts hold moisture for longer and give your plants more stability. They provide more trace elements and are good for long-term growing. The disadvantage is that they are cooler (temperature, not style) and can get waterlogged – sitting in cold, wet compost suits very few plants.

Loam- or **soil-free** compost – based on organic matter. The most popular commercial general-purpose growing media contain peat, but you can avoid this by using widely available peat-free products (see *For peat's sake* on page 221 to find out why that might be a good idea).

The advantage of a soil-free compost is that it is **lightweight**. This is important if you move your containers around frequently, if you plan to hang them up or if you keep them on a flat roof or other structure that isn't designed to bear a heavy load. (Obviously, if you live up several flights of stairs, lightweight is helpful here too.) The disadvantage is that loam-free composts dry out quickly and if they get really dry, then re-wetting them can be a struggle.

You can modify each type of compost by mixing in a proportion of the other and by adding grit, sand, leaf mould, vermiculite or perlite (minerals that open up the consistency) and fertiliser.

Make your own compost: this is a great way to recycle your vegetable food waste, cardboard packaging and plant prunings. It also helps to cut down on peat use – and, of course, plastic packaging, road miles and so on. Composting harnesses natural processes to decompose plant-based materials, resulting in a rich organic substance that you can use to top-dress your containers ('top dress' means to cover the surface of the soil) or mix with loam and grit to make your own potting medium. You can use it to improve the composts you've bought too. There are lots of methods for making it, including hot composting, cold-composting and wormeries – it's worth doing a bit of research to work out which would suit the space you have and the amount of time you've got. The materials you can compost depend on the system you choose, but as a general rule of thumb, don't compost meat or dairy products or perennial weeds.

BEWARE: home-composting is addictive.

Composts indoors As with outdoor plants, the growing medium is there to deliver water and nutrients, as well as providing stability. Different types of plants need different treatment.

Epiphytic plants – such as many bromeliad species and orchids – grow not in the soil, but instead on trees and rocks, gripping with their roots. They collect rainwater that falls onto their roots and nutrients from animal, vegetable and mineral detritus that collects and breaks down around them. The compost needed for these plants serves two purposes – to anchor the plant and to deliver sufficient water while allowing **light and air** to reach its roots. Epiphytic compost is usually a chunky loose mixture of shredded conifer bark, perlite, charcoal, and sometimes peat or coir.

Succulents need **super-sharp drainage** and their planting mix should dry out quickly after watering. Use a loam-based compost mixed with equal proportions of grit.

Carnivorous plants need a medium that is **wet** and very **low in nutrients**. These are the only plants that truly require peat (see *For peat's sake*, right). Grow them in an equal-parts mix of peat and sand, and keep it moist at all times.

Almost **all other plants** need a moist, free-draining growing medium. A **soil-based** compost can sustain **vigorous growers** for longer, and as it is heavy, will **stabilise** large-leaved plants. It is good for bulbs too. A **soil-free compost** contains much more **organic matter**, which holds onto **moisture** for longer and creates a more **humid** environment. It is good for African violets and ferns, as well as rainforest plants.

For peat's sake (a solemn rant about sustainability)

A disastrously high proportion of composts, or growing media, contain peat (sometimes known as peat moss or sphagnum peat moss). And its use is completely unnecessary.

Peat is made from partially decayed organic matter and develops over many thousands of years, in often extensive wetland areas. These peat bogs are rich enigmatic habitats for birds and insects and plants. They also lock up the greenhouse gas carbon dioxide, storing far more than all of Europe's forests.

The peat used by the horticultural industry is harvested from lowland raised bogs – damaging and often destroying these ancient habitats.

Why does this continue, when it is so unsustainable? The Royal Botanic Gardens, Kew, made the policy decision to stop using peat in 1989, except to cultivate carnivorous plants, which can't be grown in any other medium.

There are plenty of good alternatives to peat-based compost – often recycling by-products from other industries, like vegetable and forestry waste. And of course you can enrich your peat-free purchases with your very own home-made compost.

So, just say 'NO' to peat. Please.

Containers

Containers are decorative, portable and, most importantly, hold your plants in the compost that is so critical to their health.

If your plants are in containers, you can take them with you if you move to a new place. On a less momentous level, some plants love being put outside all summer and other indoor plants enjoy an **occasional outing** for a summer rain shower. Containers full of spring flowers can be moved to the side when their display is done, while the summer ones take their seasonal place in the limelight. Smaller pots can be hung from walls or raised up so you can see the glorious detail of their inhabitants. And if you're **going away**, you can group your containers together so that the wonderful person who has agreed to look after them can water them all in one go.

Essentially, the container houses the roots of your plants in the compost that's right for it. It needs to be able to retain enough water for the plant, while having holes in its base so that excess water can drain away. In general, if you're planting a single specimen, give it a container that is 5 cm (2 in) larger in diameter than its rootball (of course there are exceptions – some plants flower better when their roots are constricted, so check their needs beforehand).

But what is **the right kind of container**? As long as it is **clean** and has **drainage holes**, then you can grow a plant – or many plants – in it (be especially thorough with cleaning if it once held chemicals or foods that could contaminate the compost).

Containers are **decorative**. There's lots of recycling fun to be had – wholesale **food tins**, old **enamel bread bins**, **fruit boxes**, **baskets**. An **old tin bath** gives you ample room for vegetables or big plants like dahlias. Try flea markets, car-boot sales and charity shops. Equally, if your budget stretches to it (or someone nice asks you what you would like for your birthday), every garden centre or homeware shop will have **ceramic**, **terracotta** and **metal** containers in all shapes, sizes and colours.

The **material** your container is made of affects the way you **care** for your plants. Traditional **terracotta pots** need frequent watering in warm weather, as moisture in the compost evaporates through their sides.

Hanging baskets are extremely thirsty, as they are exposed on all sides. **Plastic or glazed containers** hold onto water for longer, as the sides are impermeable, but there is a risk of waterlogging in winter. **Stone troughs** and **wooden barrels** insulate plant roots against extremes of heat and cold, but if your yard or balcony gets very low temperatures you might want to protect terracotta and plastic containers with a layer or two of bubblewrap.

The **shape** of your container also makes a difference to your **watering** regime – compost in **wide-rimmed** containers loses more water from its surface, while containers with a **restricted** neck compared to their overall size hold onto water for longer.

To help with drainage and to stop the base of the container becoming waterlogged, **raise it up on bricks**.

Containers indoors There are two layers to indoor containers.

First there's the container that holds the compost – this must have holes in its base to drain excess water. It can be made of any material, as long as it drains. It can be a showy glazed pot or a plain plastic one.

Then there's the container that holds that excess water so it doesn't soak the floor below, or the surface it's sitting on (unless you live in a castle with stone floors that don't mind being dripped on. Or a cave, but they're usually short on light). So it needs to be watertight.

If the main container isn't good looking, you can cover it up with your outer watertight container. Otherwise, just sit the main container on a shallow dish or tray.

Watering

Plants need water. They need it first and foremost for photosynthesis. But they also need it to maintain pressure in their cells, to support their leaves and shoots, and to take up dissolved nutrients from the soil and move it around their structures.

If they're outside, they'll get rained on, right? Yes, but maybe not enough. As soon as you start growing them in containers, you restrict their roots from wandering, so their access to water is limited. And if you're growing them in a yard or on a balcony, the surrounding walls create what's known as a rain shadow, sheltering the plants from downpours. Most outdoor plants enjoy good air movement, but very windy days accelerate water loss. Finally, containers heat up faster than the earth below and if they're made of porous material they will lose moisture through their sides too.

The main enemy of indoor plants is water. Too much, to little or not the right kind. Crumbs. But it's not as challenging as it sounds. With a little observation, you'll soon get to know what your plant needs. Do check your plants regularly – indoors and outdoors – to make sure they have enough water.

So how can you tell?

You'll probably have noticed that many of the outdoor plants recommended in this book need 'moist, free-draining soil'. This might sound like a contradiction, but all it means is that while their roots need water, they also need air. Sitting in waterlogged soil effectively drowns them.

How to water From above. Using a watering can, start by watering your plant really thoroughly. That means making sure the growing medium is soaked right through to the base, not just on the surface. The surface of the compost should be about 2 cm (1 in) below the rim of the container: fill to the rim with water and gravity will pull the water down through the growing medium until it seeps out of the drainage holes. Empty any excess water that has collected in the saucer under the plant or in the outer container of indoor plants. Don't leave your plant sitting in water (unless it's a true water plant, such as a pitcher plant or a waterlily).

From below. Especially for indoor plants. Fill the drip tray with water and allow the compost to absorb it from the bottom up. Keep adding water until no more is taken up. After 20 minutes, empty out any unabsorbed water left in the saucer or outer container. Don't allow your plant to sit in excess water (unless it's a true water plant, such as a pitcher plant or a waterlily) for more than half an hour.

How often to water When the top 5 cm (2 in) of the compost feels dry (your finger is a brilliant hi-tech water gauge), it's time to water again (unless the plant is a succulent. Bear in mind that just because one container is dry, it doesn't mean all of them are. Some plants and containers use up more water than others. In very hot sunny weather, you'll find that most of your outdoor container plants need watering daily. Conversely, in winter, you might find you don't need to be watered for weeks on end.

Outside, the best time to water is early in the morning when the temperature is cooler, so the water won't immediately evaporate from the surface of the pot. Avoid wetting the foliage – in very strong sunlight, water droplets on the leaves can damage the plant tissues beneath, so direct the water at the base of the plant, where it meets the compost.

What kind of water? Tap water is treated and contains salts, minerals and chemicals that build up in your soil or compost over time and stress out your plants. The salts in tap water also tend to make it alkaline, but most plants prefer pH levels to be slightly on the acidic side – just like rainwater.

So, if you can, collect rainwater for your houseplants. The plants like it and anyway, it's more sustainable than using expensively treated tap water. Leave containers outside in the rain. Ideally, channel water from the roof of your building into a water butt (get permission first). Many plants will tolerate tap water, but orchids, bromeliads, carnivorous plants and air plants react badly. If you can't store rainwater (or have run dry), you can use cooled boiled water from the kettle for these beauties, as boiling removes some of the calcium.

How much to water
There are some basic rules that should keep your indoor vegetable companions happy. They all require the same low-tech water gauge – your index finger. If you push your finger into the compost to a depth of about 2.5 cm (1 in), you should be able to tell whether the soil is dry, moist or wet.
- **Your aim is to keep the compost moist.**
- **When you water, keep going until water drains out of the pot's base.**

> '**Lots of plants dislike the lime in our tap water, so every time I use the kettle, I boil a little bit more water than I need. I collect and cool the surplus in a large pot and use it to water my ferns, because boiling it takes out the lime, making it more acid.'**
>
> Andreas Groeger, botanist

To avoid overwatering, wait until the compost has almost dried out before watering again.

If you find a routine useful, by all means check your plants at the same intervals during the week, but don't assume they need watering each time.

Spring and summer Most plants need to be watered more often in spring and summer when they are in active growth. Even then, a period of cooler weather might slow down their water use. If you've thrown open the windows and got the air moving on a warm day they'll get thirsty, while a still, humid day might not dent their reserves.

Winter With cooler temperatures and weaker light, a plant's metabolism slows, so it requires less water. Your index finger water gauge is crucial now, to prevent overwatering.

Keeping up humidity Plants from tropical forests, like orchids, bromeliads and large-leaved plants, have adapted to raised humidity. To keep up the humidity, make a gravel reservoir: put a layer of gravel in the saucer beneath the pot and keep about 1 cm (1/3 in) of water in it at all times. This will evaporate, creating a humid microclimate around the leaves above it. This is particularly important if you keep your heating turned up high and your windows firmly closed in winter. Central heating dries out the air and can really desiccate the large leaves of plants grown for foliage.

Bromeliads have their very own reservoirs, where their leaves meet their stems. Orchids like steamy humidity, so keep their loose bark compost moist. Both orchids and bromeliads need rainwater, whenever possible.

Grouping plants together raises the humidity around them. An assemblage of different leaf shapes, colours and textures looks great too. Just remember that some plants won't appreciate being too close to their steamy cousins. Cacti and succulents thrive in the dry air that characterises their arid native habitats.

PS As epiphytes, moth orchids grow not in the soil but on trees and rocks, and are adapted to receive light on their clinging roots. The main, inner container contains the orchid compost (typically a loose, chunky bark mix), which stabilises the plant and holds in the humidity around the roots after you have watered. Use a translucent plastic pot as the inner container. Then sit it in a handsome outer pot that is a few centimetres wider, to allow light to still reach the roots.

Feeding

In their wild habitats, plants get all the nutrients they need from their surroundings – from the soil, the air and the decay of other plants around them. The woodland floor has layers of fallen leaves that slowly disintegrate, their nutrients returned to the soil by the activities of countless bacteria, fungi, invertebrates and micro-organisms. Fallen vegetation accumulates in hollows and gets caught around the base of plants on open rocky hillsides and then begins its decay.

Many indoor plants featured in this book come from tropical forests. Unlike temperate deciduous forests, the ancient soils are not very rich in nutrients – the heavy rainfall washes them out of the soil. Most of the nutrients are locked up in the living vegetation, dead wood and decaying leaves. Micro-organisms, fungi and insects recycle the decaying organic material so fast that few nutrients ever reach the soil. But there is a thin layer of decaying organic matter on the forest floor providing nutrients for herbaceous plants and shrubs.

In your yard and on your balcony, and most of all indoors, these natural processes are disrupted, so you need to supply additional nutrients to keep your plants healthy.

Most composts have added slow-release fertilisers that can be effective for a couple of months. But frequent watering washes the water-soluble nutrients out of the compost, so it's wise to top them up on a regular basis during the growing season.

Fertilisers are either organic (from animal or plant substances) or inorganic (from minerals). They come in liquid form (usually as a concentrate to be added to the watering can) or dry (pellets, granules or powders that should be mixed into the compost or applied to its surface, or dissolved in water and applied as a liquid feed). Your plants won't need feeding outside the growing season. The balance of elements in a feed promoting flowers and fruits will be different to one promoting green leafy growth. Whatever kind you choose, follow the manufacturer's instructions carefully. More is not better – if you apply fertiliser in too high a concentration or too frequently, it could damage your plants.

Loam-based composts have more trace elements and nutrients than loam-free (see *Composts* on page 220), so plants grown in the former need less feeding.

The long and the short of it is: feed your plants in the growing season, don't feed your plants outside the growing season, and repot them every year into fresh compost to replenish the nutrients taken up or watered out in the previous growing season. If the container is very large, you can simply replace the top 10–15 cm (4–6 in) with fresh compost (known as top-dressing).

PS Succulents and cacti are slow growing, thanks to their crassulacean acid metabolism (see *Succulent survivors* on page 116). They don't need as much feeding as more leafy plants. During the growing season, apply a balanced fertiliser, at half the recommended dosage rate, no more than once a month.

Potting on

Plants grow. Some of them fast and some of them slow. But whatever the rate, increased volume above ground means the roots are growing too, gradually occupying the entire container.

If a plant is too pot-bound – meaning its root system has filled the container – it is likely to dry out quickly. And if there's no more room for root growth, there is unlikely to be much further growth of the whole plant.

Some plants respond to being pot-bound in a way that suits their human companion. If the roots of a spider plant (see *Retro* on page 103) are a little bit squeezed, it will put out feelers with plantlets on the end of them, ready to root when they touch down in a less confined spot. A peace lily (see photo on page 210) produces flowers more readily if its roots are a bit squashed.

But if you want your plant to grow, sooner or later you'll need to pot it on, which means transferring it to a larger pot.

- Take the pot with the plant in it and lie it carefully on its side.
- Trim any roots emerging from the drainage holes.

- Shake or tap the pot a few times and the plant and rootball should slide from the container.
- Use your fingers to gently pull any entangled roots apart, taking care not to snap them off.
- Prepare a new pot – its diameter should only be about 5 cm (2 in) larger than the old one.
- Put a layer of pebbles or broken terracotta into the bottom of the pot to ensure good drainage.

- Cover the drainage layer with compost suitable for the plant, so that once the rootball is placed on top, its surface is about 2.5 cm (1 in) below the rim of the pot.
- Make sure the rootball is central in the pot, and fill any gaps with compost, firming in well with your hands.
- Water the plant generously and allow to drain.

Look after your leaves

'You can buy special wipes to clean tropical foliage plants, but I just use an ordinary cleaning cloth for my Swiss cheese plant. I also mist the leaves regularly. Central heating makes homes a bit dry, and misting the plants raises the humidity.'

Chris Brown, student gardener, Kew

A leaf surface gathers dust, just like every other surface in your home.

But while the rest of your space can be as dusty as the surface of the moon, spare a little time to keep your indoor plants dust-free.

The reason? Plants derive their energy from light. If there's a layer of dust blocking its path, they will struggle.

You can give your big-leaved foliage plants and palms an occasional shower. Literally. Stand them in the shower tray and spray them over with tepid water. Even better, if the weather's warm, leave them out in the rain for half an hour.

In between showers, cup the leaf with your hand and remove dust from the top surface with a soft damp cloth. (Be sure not to use one that might have household chemical residues on it.)

Plants with delicate foliage, such as ferns, can be cleaned by misting them with water from a fine spray.

Hairy leaves – such as the velvety foliage of African violets – aren't able to shed water like their smooth-leaved cousins. If they do need a clean, just spray them. Then turn the plant on its side and give it a few sharp taps to remove excess water, so it doesn't form pools on the leaves.

You'd get in a bit of a pickle if you tried to dust a cactus with a fine soft cloth. Instead use a soft makeup or shaving brush or even a feather duster to give it a spruce up.

Is there a doctor in the house?

In the case of most common indoor plant problems, the symptoms are in the leaves.

Limp leaves The symptoms of overwatering and underwatering are very similar in leafy plants: an exhausted appearance, with limp leaves and stems. To make your diagnosis, you need to check the pot!

- Is there surplus water in the saucer underneath it? If so, pour it out.
- Is the compost soggy? Maybe you're watering too much. Ease off, watering only when the compost has dried out to a depth of several centimetres.
- Is the compost very dry? Perhaps you're not watering it enough. Once the compost has got very dry, it can become almost water repellent, so when you water, it simply runs down between the compost and the side of the pot, bypassing the poor plant's root system all together.

Yellow leaves This could be caused by overfeeding, overwatering or a draughty location.

Brown leaf tips or shrivelling leaves Several different possible causes: overly dry air (raise the humidity using a pebble tray – see *Keeping up humidity* page 225), overwatering or underwatering, pot-bound roots, or draughts. Check carefully to ensure you make the right diagnosis, so you can prescribe the right treatment.

Mouldy leaves Downy mildew causes a fuzzy mould on the underside of leaves and is a sign that a plant is cold and damp (so move it to a warmer place. Powdery mildew (a white powdery fungus) is caused by a combination of dry roots and poor ventilation.

Nibbled leaves Notches taken out of the leaf edges are a sign of vine weevils. The damage caused by the adult beetles isn't too extensive. However, where there's an adult vine weevil, sure as eggs is eggs the larvae will follow. These small white grubs with orange heads hatch in the compost and munch their way through plant roots (primroses and their relatives are particular favourites). One day the plant looks healthy, the next you can lift it straight off the soil without resistance, as the roots have been eaten away. Grrr. So if you catch sight of a weevil (like a leggy beetle with a long snout) hanging around your plants, politely ask it to leave. And if you come across the grubs in the compost, squash them (if your karma allows you to).

Pruning and deadheading

To prune or not to prune

Pruning is an impressive **art**. For more than a thousand years it's been taken to great heights by bonsai masters (who can be women too, by the way). Through precise pruning, they manipulate the balance of growth hormones in their trees, coaxing them into miniature forms of their natural full-sized selves. Amazing. You should try it. (Obsession alert: can become all-consuming.)

And then there are the **fantastical shapes** of yew trees, clipped box hedging and wall-trained shrubs that have been all the rage with European royalty over the past few centuries.

But it's not all just for show. Canny pruning improves the fruit crop on trees and bushes. It can encourage flowers rather than leafy growth, increase air-flow and improve a plant's stability. Crucially, for those of us who like to stay nimble, it also limits the size of plants. So you can move house and take your precious vegetable companions with you without having to call in the heavies.

For our purposes, pruning is about keeping plants:

- **healthy** – removing dead or diseased plant material.
- **handsome** – removing old flower spikes and damaged leaves.
- **handy** – trimming them to fit your space or keep them portable.

In general, if you're removing a branch or reducing the length of a stem, always cut just above a **node**. Nodes are found at intervals along the stem and it is from these points that leaves and side shoots are produced. If a plant has got very leggy, with all its leaves at the top or end of the stem, you can usually spot lower nodes by the scar where a leaf or shoot once was or by a raised thickening of the stem (think of the sections of a piece of bamboo – the thicker rings along the cane are the nodes).

Roses, bougainvilleas and **fuchsias** flower on the new season's growth, so prune them in spring, just as the buds begin to sprout new leaves and shoots. You're aiming for a balanced, open structure for good air circulation, so they don't get hot and bothered on humid summer days. Remove weak and damaged stems and shorten all stems to a strong framework. You'll be amazed how quickly the plant will extend and fill out.

Indoors, prune dumb cane (*Dieffenbachia seguine*) and Swiss cheese plants (*Monstera*), jade plants (*Crassula*), bougainvilleas and tradescantia to limit their size.

Whenever you prune, it's important to make clean cuts. This minimises the surface area of the wound, making it easier for the plant to heal. So use a sharp knife or scissors or secateurs (health and safety alert) to avoid tearing the plant tissue. By removing a section of stem above a node, you can prompt the plant to sprout leaves or shoots from that node.

Some dead or damaged plant material will just fall away from the plant with gentle persuasion, but if it's persistent and looks like it's spreading, cut into the living tissue below it – the wound will callus over (form thickened tissue that prevents dehydration) and healing will begin.

Warning: palm trees mustn't be pruned. They have a single growing tip, and if it's removed, then it's game over. But you can remove individual leaves if they die, cutting them off at the base.

Deadheading

Deadhead to keep those flowers coming all summer.

It sounds like something out of a zombie flick, but deadheading actually helps your plants to keep on blooming.

Plants flower in order to reproduce: the end game is the production of seeds. These are then dispersed and grow into new plants. Once a flower forms, the plant directs its energy into the production of seedheads, nuts or fruits. The display of flowers fades and growth slows down.

So if you remove the flowers (not just the petals but the entire flowerhead, including the swollen tissue underneath the flower), the plant will continue to put its energy into blooming.

Lots of herbaceous plants (plants that die down each winter) and annuals (plants that germinate, grow and die in the same year) benefit from deadheading. Also remove the flowers of bedding plants – pansies, petunias, busy Lizzies – by pinching out the tops of the stems with your fingertips. You might need scissors or secateurs for roses and perennials, such as pelargoniums, ox-eye daisies and dahlias.

Of course, removing flowers as they fade also keeps your display looking beautiful. Petals that fall in clumps onto leaves on still, humid days sometimes start their decay where they land, and can encourage mildew on your plants. Best to remove them.

'If you're interested in trying bonsai, the best plants to start with are seedlings of Japanese maples (*Acer palmatum* and cultivars). They are cheap to buy, readily available, have small leaves and respond well to bonsai pruning techniques.'

Richard Kernick, bonsai specialist, Kew

Share

There are lots of ways of sharing plants – some of them produce plantlets or offsets that you can pot up, others can be divided. But you can also actively propagate them. Your gift problems solved forever!

Sowing seeds and taking cuttings
One of the most exciting things about getting plants is sowing seeds. If you're short of space, this is your chance to have trees! If you're short of cash, this is the way to surround yourself with plants. If you're short of gifts for your friends, this is the route to presents that will be treasured. More than anything, it's amazing to watch a seed you've sown become a flourishing plant.

A seed is extraordinary. A little package containing an embryonic plant and a food store that will support it until it's able to support itself through its roots and shoots. It can be a millimetre in size, like the seed of a poppy, or 4 cm (1½ in) long, like an avocado stone, or weigh more than 1 kg (2 lb), like a coconut.

You need to give it the right conditions for germination. Some seeds will only germinate after a

'Autumn was all about conkers, so the first plant I grew from seed was a horse chestnut tree. I still grow trees from seed – horse chestnuts, oaks, cedars. If you grow them in air pots – cylinders with perforated sides – their roots don't spiral, so when you transplant them into open ground after a few years, they establish really well.'

Will Harding, arborist, Kew

period of cold. Others need to be soaked in water. Some even need fire! This makes sense when you think about what a seedling requires in order to survive. A seed that needs a cold period has adapted to germinate only when winter is over, so the resulting seedling has the warm, light growing season ahead of it. A seed that needs to be soaked in water will germinate when there is enough water to support the growing plant. And once fire has destroyed the existing habitat, a new seedling will have far less competition for light, water and nutrients.

The basics:
Make your own pot or seedtray using a plastic container such as a soft fruit container or yoghurt pot. Just puncture the base to make sure of good drainage.

Fill the container with compost and firm it gently. Prepared seed compost is fine and free draining. **Spread** the seeds very sparsely over the surface and cover with a thin layer of compost. Sow large seeds singly or in pairs in a pot. **Sit** the container in a tray of water and it will take up all the moisture it needs. Then remove and allow to drain.

Position the container in the right place: some seeds need warmth, others are happy outside on a windowsill. Some seeds germinate better in raised humidity, in which case you can put the pot in a sealed plastic bag, but as soon as the seedlings appear, take the pot out again to deter fungal diseases.

Water regularly with a very fine rose on the watering can or use a spray mister – don't water in a powerful torrent, as it may well eject the seeds and compost from the container! You can also continue to sit the container in a tray to water from below.

Prick out the seedlings: if you have sown lots of seeds into a tray, there will come a point when you need to pot on the strongest seedlings into individual pots, to grow them on either for planting in containers outside or for display indoors. When a seedling is large enough to handle, grip its leaves gently (not its stem) and carefully dig its delicate roots out of the tray. Create a hole in the compost of its new container, feed its roots into the hole, and position it so that its first leaves are just above the surface of the compost. Water it from the top, so that the compost settles snugly around its roots.

Hardening off: if your seedling is destined for life outside, gradually acclimatise it to cooler conditions by giving it outings during the day. Then leave it outside in a sheltered place – perhaps in a box with a pane of glass or plastic on top – and only after a few weeks introduce it to its final place of glory.

'My first plant was the spider plant that I grew in my bedroom. I was fascinated by the way it put out new plantlets, making it really easy to propagate.'

Joe Clements,
student gardener, Kew

Taking cuttings

If you want more exact replicas of your favourite plant.
If you're short of cash and you want to bulk up your summer displays.
If you want to get tender plants through the winter.
If you simply want to share the joy.

This process produces clones of the parent plant. It takes advantage of the extraordinary ability plants have to produce roots at the base of wounded stems. Essentially, the stem of the parent plant is cut off and planted in damp compost. After a few weeks, *hey presto*! The cutting produces new roots and a new plant establishes.

Pelargoniums (see *Trashy* on page 60) are brilliant plants for developing your skills. One strong pelargonium bought from a shop in early spring can translate into windowboxes billowing with bright flowers two months later or lovely gifts to share with your friends. Cuttings taken in spring are known as softwood cuttings. And your pelargoniums keep on giving – you can take cuttings from the same plants in late summer, to maintain them indoors through

'Sharing is caring! It's always better to swap plants with other people, as their plants are already used to the environment at home, whereas nursery-grown plants could struggle if not acclimatised properly.'

Rebecca Hilgenhof, tender plants specialist, Kew

the winter without taking up too much space. These are known as semi-ripe cuttings – shrubby herbs such as rosemary and lavender can also be propagated in this way.

Softwood cuttings: in spring, take 8 cm (3 in) lengths of the new growth of the plant, ideally with two or three leaves. If there are already flower buds on the stem, remove them by pinching them out. Fill a 9 cm (3½ in) plastic pot with a mixture of one part multi-purpose compost to one part grit or perlite. Make a hole in the compost with a pencil, and insert the cutting right up to the first leaf. Water it in.

The cutting will continue to lose water through its leaves, and until it has produced roots it will be unable to replace it. To minimise water loss, keep the humidity high around the cutting by covering it with a hood of clear plastic or spraying it frequently for the first few days. Once the cutting has rooted, pot it into a richer compost. Plant it outside after hardening off (see page 233).

Semi-ripe cuttings: in late summer, select several healthy side shoots with two or three leaves, about 8 cm (3 in) long. Pull each side shoot away from the main stem, detaching it from the parent plant. Fill a 15 cm (6 in) plastic pot with a mixture of one part multi-purpose compost to one part grit or perlite. Insert several shoots into the compost (spaced around the edge) and keep it watered until roots develop. Once the cuttings have rooted, they can be overwintered on a well-lit indoor windowsill. Water them sparingly in winter, allowing the compost to dry out between waterings.

In mid-spring, re-pot overwintered plants/cuttings into a richer multi-purpose compost

'I first got interested in plants when I was really young. We cut a flower stem from a flowering currant and put it in a vase and it grew roots. So I potted it up. A case of unintentional propagation. I was amazed.'

Richard Kernick, bonsai specialist, Kew

with added grit, pinching out the shoot tips to encourage bushy growth. Place them outside once the risk of frost has passed and

they will repay your care with another fantastic display all summer long.

Appendix

Latin names of the plants that star in each photograph.

Page 8 Pincushion flower *Scabiosa* 'Butterfly Blue Beauty'

Page 10 *Dahlia* 'Dalina Maxi Topia'

Page 11 *Tradescantia zebrina*

Page 14 *Gymnocalycium pflanzii, Sarracenia* Juthatip Soper x *Sarracenia leucophylla, Austroyclindropuntia subulata*

Page 16 *Carex* 'Ice Dance'

Page 17 Lambs lettuce *Valerianella locusta* seedlings being potted on

Page 20 Frosted ivy *Hedera helix* cultivar

Page 24 Peacock plant *Calathea* 'Medaillon'

Page 26 Elephant's ear *Alocasia* 'Black Velvet'; red bracts of *Anthurium andraeanum* 'Red Winner'

Page 27 Paint-splash effect of dumb cane *Dieffenbachia exotica* 'Compacta'; undulate margins of *Hosta* cultivar

Page 28 Pink bracts of urn plant, *Aechmea fasciata*

Page 29 Fascinating foliage of urn plant *Aechmea fasciata*; bromeliad species *Catopsis berteroniana* growing on red mangroves, *Rhizophora mangle.* Everglades National Park, Florida, USA (photo: Rebecca Hilgenhof)

Page 30 Dragon tree *Dracaena marginata* (left) and Areca palm, *Dypsis lutescens*; Kentia palms, *Howea forsteriana* growing on Lord Howe Island, credit William J Baker, Royal Botanic Gardens, Kew

Page 31 Left, parlour palm *Chamaedorea elegans*; right, umbrella tree *Schefflera actinophylla.*

Page 32 Rainforest climbers, including *Philodendron squamiferum*, Kaw Mt, French Guiana, Photo credit: Rebecca Hilgenhof

Page 33 Spider plant *Chlorophytum comosum* with abseiling spiderettes and trailing devil's ivy *Epipremnum aureum*; top right, heart-leaf plant *Philodendron scandens*; below right, flowers of jasmine *Jasminum polyanthum*

Page 34 Strawberries *Fragaria x ananassa* and lettuce *Lactuca sativa*

Page 36 Cordon tomato *Solanum lycopersicum* cultivar

Page 37 Chilli pepper *Capsicum annuum* cultivar

Page 39 Varieties of lettuce *Lactuca sativa*

Page 40 Tomatoes *Solanum lycopersicum*

Page 41 Chilli peppers *Capsicum annuum*

Page 43 Strawberries *Fragaria x ananassa*

Page 44 Maidenhair fern *Adiantum* sp.

Page 46 Daffodils *Narcissus pseudonarcissus.* (photo: Andreas Groeger)

Page 47 Left, hyacinth *Hyacinthus orientalis* 'Aida', and right, *Tulipa* 'Abu Hassan'

Page 48-49 Daffodil *Narcissus jonquilla* 'Pipit'

Page 50 Hart's tongue fern *Asplenium scolopendrium*

Page 51 *Below left,* Boston fern *Nephrolepis exaltata*

Page 52 Moth orchid *Phalaenopsis* cultivar with the tropical climber devil's ivy *Epipremnum aureum*

Page 53 Moth orchid *Phalaenopsis deliciosa* in Laos (photo: Andre Schuiteman)

Page 54 Rose cultivar *Rosa* 'Anne Boleyn'

Page 55 Left, bougainvillea cultivar *Bougainvillea x buttiana*; orange hibiscus cultivar *Hibiscus rosa-sinensis* cultivar

Page 56 Cockscomb *Celosia* Kimono *series*

Page 58-59 Orange and red *Begonia x tuberhybrida* and deep pink *Pelargonium* cultivars

Page 60 Pelargonium species, Table Mountain, Cape Town, South Africa (photo: Richard Wilford)

Page 61 Pink pelargonium *Pelargonium* 'Dark Caliente Pink'

Page 62-63 Three dahlia cultivars: *Dahlia* 'Dalia Maxi Topia' (red); *Dahlia* 'Mystic Spirit' (orange); *Dahlia* 'Mystic Illusion' (yellow)

Page 64 Purple and yellow pinwheels *Petunia* 'Banoffee Pie'; pink and yellow pinwheels *Petunia* 'Heartbreaker'

Page 65 Deep purple *Petunia* 'Black Velvet'

Page 66 Cockscomb *Celosia* Kimono series

Page 67 Cockscomb *Celosia* 'Deep Purple'; bedding begonia cultivars *Begonia x tuberhybrida* Front left, Snapdragon cultivar *Antirrhinum majus* 'Floral Showers Apricot bicolor' and, front right, *Celosia* 'Deep Purple', *Dianthus* 'Oscar'

Page 68 Flowers of the field: blue love-in-the-mist *Nigella damascena*; orange poppy *Papaver rupifragum*; ox-eye daisy *Leucanthemum vulgare*

Page 70 Many tiny pink flowers of *Thymus sibthorpii*

Page 71 Lavender *Lavandula multifida* in its rocky dry habitat in Almeria, Spain (photo: Tony Hall); sage *Salvia officinalis* and thyme *Thymus vulgaris* with the grass-like foliage of chives *Allium schoenoprasum* and mint *Mentha x piperita* in the background

Page 72 Blue aster *Symphyotrichum novi-belgii* 'Blue Lagoon'

Page 73 Above, African daisy cultivar *Osteospermum cv*; below, mountain meadow in the Dolomites, Italy (photo: Katherine Price)

Page 74-75 Forget-me-not *Myosotis sylvatica*

Page 76 Grass species dominate an ancient wet meadow in the Austrian Alps (photo: Katherine Price); the dainty flower sprays of wood melick *Melica uniflora*

Page 77 Stripy sedge *Carex morrowii* 'Ice Dance'; spiky blue fescue *Festuca glauca*

Page 78 Pitcher plant *Sarracenia minor*

Page 80 Pitcher plant *Sarracenia flava* growing by a lake in Sandhills, North Carolina, USA (photo: Katherine Price)

Page 81 Pitcher plant *Sarracenia flava* hybrid, Venus flytrap *Dionaea muscipula*

Page 82-83 Pitcher plant *Sarracenia flava* hybrid

Page 84 Three species of living stones (clockwise from left) *Lithops lesliei f.albinica, Lithops salicola, Lithops bromfieldii var. mennellii*

Page 85 Many genera in the family Mesembryanthemaceae (Aizoaceae), including *Lithops*, originate in the dry lands of Southern Africa

Page 86 Top to bottom, *Tillandsia fasciculata, T. brachycaulos, T. mauryana*; *Tillandsia* species colonising telegraph wires in Venezuela (photo: Andreas Groeger)

Page 87 Left to right: *Tillandsia juncea, T. ionantha* 'Rubra', *T. ionantha stricta*

Page 88 Purple *Primula* 'Joanne' and red *Primula* 'Scorcher'

Page 90 Primroses *Primula vulgaris* and violets *Viola odorata* growing wild on a woody slope in Hampshire, UK (photo: Katherine Price)

Page 91 *Polyanthus* 'Crescendo Golden' and blue forget-me-not *Myosotis sylvatica*

Page 92 Pansy *Viola tricolor* var *hortensis* cv

Page 93 *Viola* cultivar

Page 94 Clockwise, from left: Snapdragon cultivar *Antirrhinum majus* 'Floral Showers Apricot bicolor', *Celosia* 'Deep Purple', *Dianthus* 'Oscar'

Page 96 African violet *Saintpaulia ionantha*

Page 97 Florist's cyclamen *Cyclamen persicum*; and *Cyclamen coum* in its native woodland habitat, Republic of Georgia (photo: Richard Wilford)

Page 98 *Fuchsia* 'Lady Thumb'

Page 100 Mother-in-law's tongue *Sansevieria trifasciata*

Page 101 Aspidistra *Aspidistra elatior*

Page 102 *Fuchsia* 'Lady Thumb'

Page 103 Left, spiderwort *Tradescantia zebrina*; airplant *Tillandsia ionantha stricta*, spider plant *Chlorophytum comosum* 'Vittatum', maidenhair fern *Adiantum fragrans*

Page 104–105 Sunflower *Helianthus* 'Sunsation'

Page 106 Rubber tree *Ficus elastica*

Page 107 Swiss cheese plant *Monstera deliciosa*

Page 108 Clockwise from top, *Echinocactus sp. Agave gypsophila, Agave guadalajarana,* black pot of *Agave* seedlings, *Lophophora williamsii, Agave victoriae-reginae, Echinopsis spachiana* (columnar cactus, centre), *Haworthia truncata*

Page 109–110 Left to right, *Pelargonium x ardens,* twining climber *Jasminum sambac,* unidentified cactus, slender spikes of *Aloe vera,* spiny *Aloe brevifolia,* blue rosettes of *Echeveria glauca,* small Crimson flowers of *Pelargonium sidoides*

Page 112 Houseleek *Sempervivum montanum* in the Swiss Alps (photo: Joanne Everson)

Page 113 Top left, houseleek cultivars *Sempervivum* cultivar; bottom left, *Sedum furfuraceum*; right, *Echeveria glauca* flanked by *Aloe ferox* (left) and *Pelargonium* 'Ardens'

Page 114 Left (left to right), unidentified cactus, *Echinopsis spachiana, Lophophora williamsii, Agave gypsophila*; barrel cactus *Ferocactus sp,* King Canyon, Saguaro National Park, Arizona USA (photo: Maia Ross)

Page 115 Below, Saguaro cactus *Carnegiea gigantea,* Saguaro National Park, Arizona USA (photo: Maia Ross); top, left to right, *Cleistocactus, Oreocereus, Cleistocactus, Mammillaria coahuilensis*

Page 116 South African landscape (photo: Paul Rees)

Page 117 Left, haworthia *Haworthia pumila* with *Haworthia cymbiformis* (below) and *Haworthia attenuata* (above); right, aloe *Aloe brevifolia* (middle) with Arabian jasmine *Jasminum sambac* (above) and *Echeveria glauca* (right).

Page 121 Border auriculas *Auricula* 'Finley' and blue *Auricula* 'Alison Rose'

Page 122 Cosmos *Cosmos* 'Carmine Sonata'

Page 125 Bougainvillea cultivar *Bougainvillea x buttiana*

Page 127 Top left (left to right), pink and white *Dianthus barbatus* 'Barbarini Red Picotee', ox-eye daisy *Leucanthemum vulgare*, English rose *Rosa* 'Anne Boleyn'; top right, orange *Dahlia* 'Mystic Spirit', bushy orange *Chrysanthemum* 'Conaco Orange', silver grass Miscanthus sinensis 'Adagio'; bottom right sunflower cultivar *Helianthus* 'Sunsation'

Page 128 Japanese painted fern *Athyrium nipponicum* var. *pictum,* stripy sedge *Carex morrowii* 'Ice Dance', oriental lily *Lilium orientale* 'Maru', shield fern *Polystichum* 'Jade' and, rear, *Fatsia japonica*; *Anemanthele lessoniana* (formerly *Stipa arundinacea*), *Echeveria* cultivar, bronze form of *Carex comans*

Page 129 *Hosta* 'Marilyn Monroe', left, and *Hosta* 'Great Expectations'

Page 130 *Tulipa* 'Abu Hassan'

Page 131 *Rosa* 'Parade Neza'

Page 132 Cultivars of autumn-flowering cyclamen *Cyclamen hederifolium*

Page 133 Left, red sepals and clashing purple petals of cultivar *Fuchsia* 'Bella'; right, *Petunia* 'Surfina Purple', scarlet pelargonium *Pelargonium* cultivar

Page 134 *Pelargonium* 'Avenida Red', *Dahlia* 'Dalina Maxi Topia'

Page 136 Clockwise from left, foliage of coleus *Plectranthus scutellarioides* 'Dark Chocolate', sunflower *Helianthus* 'Sunsation', *Impatiens* cultivar, *Celosia* Kimono series, purple and yellow *Petunia* 'Banoffee Pie'; pink and yellow *Petunia* 'Amore Queen of Hearts'

Page 137 Clockwise from bottom left, busy Lizzy, *Impatiens* 'Magnum Pink', *Begonia semperflorens* 'Ascot Bronze Scarlet', *Dahlia* 'Bishop of Llandaff', *Fuchsia triphylla* 'Thalia', *Salvia farinacea* 'Victoria'

Page 138 Left to right, spiky fescue *Festuca glauca* 'Intense Blue', marguerite *Argyranthemum frutescens*, perennial wallflower *Erysimum* 'Bowles Mauve', French lavender *Lavandula stoechas* 'Provencal' and pincushion flower *Scabiosa* 'Butterfly Blue Beauty'

Page 139 Left to right, pheasant's tail grass *Anemanthele lessoniana*, dark rosettes of the tree aeonium *Aeonium arboreum* 'Zwartkop', encrusted rosettes of *Saxifraga longifolia x callosa* in a bowl with mixed houseleek *Sempervivum* cultivars, marguerite *Argyranthemum frutescens*

Page 140–141 Oriental lily *Lilium orientale* 'Maru'

Page 142 Lettuce *Lactuca sativa*

Page 143 Left, busy Lizzy *Impatiens hawkeri* 'Infinity Dark Pink'; right, *Polyanthus* 'Crescendo Golden', blue forget-me-not *Myosotis sylvatica*, wood melick, a shade-loving grass, *Melica uniflora*

Page 146 Succulent *Aeonium arboreum Atropurpureum*

Page 147 Miniature daffodil *Narcissus cyclamineus* cultivar

Page 148 Left, *Hosta* 'Barbara Ann' and right, *Hosta sieboldiana* cultivar

Page 149 Clockwise from left, primrose *Primula vulgaris,* lily-of-the-valley *Convallaria majalis,* purple spike of bugle *Ajuga reptans,* sweet violet *Viola odorata*

Page 150 *Pelargonium* 'Calliope Dark Red'

Page 152 *Pelargonium* 'Dark Caliente Pink'

Page 153 Above left, daffodil *Narcissus jonquilla* 'Pipit' under planted with pansies *Viola tricolor* var. *hortensis* cultivars; below left, *Cyclamen hederifolium* cultivar; right, pink bedding begonia *Begonia x benariensis* cultivar, scarlet tuberous begonia *Begonia x tuberhybrida* cultivar, trailing pelargonium *Pelargonium peltatum* cultivar

Page 154 Blue-green rosettes of *Sedum glaucophyllum*, with *Sempervivum ciliosum* (bottom left) and purple *Sedum furfuraceum*

Page 155 Left, orange *Tulipa* 'Ballerina'; right, orange *Begonia x tuberhybrida* cultivar

Page 156–157 Blue aster *Symphyotrichum novi-belgii* 'Blue Lagoon'

Page 158 Auricula cultivars, left to right, *Primula* 'Joanne', *Primula* 'Scorcher', *Primula* 'Star Wars'

Page 159 Left, *Impatiens hawkeri* cultivar; right, *Primula vulgaris* cultivar

Page 161 Clockwise from left: *Fittonia albivenis* (cutting in jar), *Sarracenia* 'Juthatip Soper' x *Sarracenia leucophylla, Calathea lanceolata, Philodendron erubescens* 'Red Emerald', *Asplenium* cultivar in white pot, *Guzmania lingulata* 'Variegata', *Sansevieria trifasciata* 'Laurentii'

Page 162 *Echeveria* cultivars, trailing *Sedum morganianum* and both green and purple forms of *Aeonium arboreum*

Page 164 *Jasminum sambac* in bud over stocky cactus, slender *Aloe vera* and the toothed *Aloe brevifolia*

Page 165 Airplant *Tillandsia capitata*

Page 166 *Mammillaria sp., Echinocactus sp., Cleistocactus sp., Mammillaria sp.*

Page 167 below, *Lithops salicola*

Page 168 *Haworthia cymbiformis*

Page 169 *Right, Phalaenopsis* cultivar, *Anthurium andraeanum* 'Red Winner'

Page 170 Mistletoe cactus *Rhipsalis baccifera*

Page 172 Clockwise from left, *Tillandsia chiapensis, T. crocata, T. fasciculata, T. mauryana, T. brachycaulos, T. funckiana*

Page 173 String-of-beads *Senecio rowleyanus*

Page 174 Hanging up: the tumbling foliage of *Peperomia prostrata,* handsome large-leaved *Alocasia regindula,* and several orchids *Cuitlauzina pendula, Bulbophyllum orthosepalum, Sievekingia reichenbachiana*

Page 175 Left, *Philodendron scandens;* right (from left), *Adiantum fragrans, Tillandsia ionantha* var. *stricta, Chlorophytum comosum* 'Vittatum'

Page 176 *Sansevieria trifasciata* 'Laurentii'

Page 178 Parlour palm *Chamaedorea elegans*

Page 179 Left, *Aspidistra lurida;* Left, *Beaucarnea recurvata* (left), *Hyophorbe lagenicaulis* (rear), *Crassula ovata* (right)

Page 180 Left to right, *Howea forsteriana, Calathea lanceolata, Calathea* 'Medaillon'

Page 182 Trailing *Sedum morganianum* with *Echeveria glauca*

Page 183 Left, *Gymnocalycium pflanzii, Sarracenia* 'Juthatip Soper' x *S. leucophylla;* right, *Kalanchoe blossfeldiana* 'Flaming Katy', *Aspidistra elatior* (rear)

Page 184 Left (left to right), *Calathea leopardina, C. rufibarba, Tradescantia pallida* 'Purple Heart'; right (left to right) *Haworthia pumila, H. limifolia, Haworthia.* 'Striata'

Page 185 *Alocasia wentii*

Page 186 Left, *Dieffenbachia exotica* 'Compacta' and, right, *Adiantum fragrans*

Page 188 *Rhipsalis baccifera*

Page 189 Left, *Phalaenopsis* cultivar; right top, *Rhipsalis* sp.; right bottom, *Tradescantia pallida* cultivar, *Chlorophytum comosum* 'Vittatum'

Page 190 Left, *Dieffenbachia exotica* 'Compacta' and, right, *Adiantum fragrans*

Page 191 Blue star fern *Phlebodium aureum*

Page 192 Clockwise from top right: *Vanda* orchid, Spanish moss *Tillandsia usneoides,* pineapple *Ananas bracteatus, Phalaenopsis* 'Panda', *Amorphophallus* 'Konjac' and, on the suspended branch, airplant *Tillandsia funckiana*

Page 194 Left to right, chilli pepper *Capsicum annuum* 'Loco', Moroccan mint *Mentha spicata* var. *crispa* 'Morroccan', basil *Ocimum basilicum*

Page 195 Left (from left), right *Mammillaria dixanthocentron, M. elongata, M. schiedeana* ssp. *giselae;* right, *Aloe vera*

Page 196 Left to right, *Crassula ovata* 'Gollum', *C. arborescens* ssp. *undulatifolia, C. ovata*

Page 197 Top left, Easter cactus *Hatiora gaertneri;* bottom left, *Begonia rex* cultivar; right, *Vriesea splendens* cultivar

Page 198 *Hydrophorbe lagenicaulis,* left, and *Ficus lyrata*

Page 200 Left to right: *Beaucarnea recurvata, Crassula ovata, Hyophorbe lagenicaulis, Ficus lyrata*

Page 201 Left, *Hippeastrum* hybrid; right, *Sarracenia* 'Juthatip Soper' x *Sarracenia leucophylla*

Page 202-203 Left to right, hairy *Echeveria setosa, Echeveria* cultivar, *Aloe variegata* (stripy), *Echeveria agavoides,* flowering *Echeveria glauca,* stripy *Haworthia attenuata, Dudleya brittonii, Echeveria glauca;* top shelf, *Echeveria* cultivars flanking stripy *Gasteria* cultivar

Page 204 *Alocasia* 'Polly'

Page 205 Left (front to back), *Crassula ovata, Calathea lanceolata, Monstera deliciosa* and on shelf, *Rhipsalis* sp.; right, *Guzmania lingulata*

Page 206 *Dracaena marginata* (left) and *Dypsis lutescens*

Page 207 *Ficus elastica*

Page 208 Front row: *Mammillaria camptotricha* 'Curvispina', *Mammillaria carmenae talbiflora, Echinocactus grusonii* var. *albispinus*

Page 210 Left to right, *Asplenium scolopendrium* 'Angustifolia', *Spathiphyllum* 'Sweet Silvio', *Kalanchoe blossfeldiana* 'Flaming Katy', *Tradescantia pallida* cultivar

Page 211 *Cyclamen persicum* cultivar

Page 212-213 *Tillandsia harrisii, T. ionantha* var. *stricta*

Page 214 *Saintpaulia ionantha*

Page 215 Top, *Begonia rex* cultivar (left), with *Zamioculcas zamiifolia;* bottom, maidenhair fern *Adiantum fragrans*

Index

Photographs are represented by page numbers in italic text.

Acer palmatum (Japanese maple) 231
Aeonium (aeonium) 112–13, *139*, *146*, *147*, *162*, *183*
African violet *(Saintpaulia)* 89, *96*, 196, *214*, 221, 228
air plant *(Tillandsia)* 79, *86–7*, *172*, *173*, *193*, *204–5*, 211, 225
Allium (chives/ornamental onion) 47, *71*
Alocasia (elephant's ear) *26–7*, *174*, *185*, *204*
Aloe (aloe) *109*, 113, 116, *117*, *164*, *194–5*, *196*, 203
Anthemis tinctoria (yellow chamomile) 72
Anthurium (flamingo flower) *26–7*, 168, *169*, 196, 211
Antirrhinum (snapdragon) *94*, 95
areca palm *(Dypsis lutescens)* *30–1*, *204*, *206*
Argyranthemum (marguerite) 72–3, *139*, 147
Aspidistra (aspidistra) 99, *100–1*, *178*, *179*, *183*, 184
Aster x frikartii (Michaelmas daisy) 72–3, 155, *156*
auricula (*Primula* hybrid) *88*, 89, *90–1*, *121*, *158*, *159*

Beaucarnea (pony tail palm, elephant's foot) 31, *179*, *200*
begonia,
    bedding *137*, *153*
    Rex cultivars (*Begonia rex* cv.) *27*, *197*, *215*
    tuberous (*Begonia x tuberhybrida*) *58–9*, *66–7*, 133, *153*, 155
blue fescue *(Festuca glauca)* *76–7*, 138
bonsai 230–1
Bougainvillea *54–5*, *125*, 167, 230
bridal wreath *(Stephanotis floribunda)* 33, *175*, *204*
bromeliad *28–9*, *86–7*, 196, *197*, *205*, 221, 225
bulb *45–7*, 126
busy Lizzie *(Impatiens)* 95, *137*, *143*, *159*, 231
button fern *(Pellaea)* *214*

cactus *108*, 114–15, *164*, 166, 167, 219, 228
    barrel *114*
    Christmas *(Schlumbergera)* 115, *214*
    Easter *(Hatiora)* 115, 196, *197*, 214
    mistletoe *(Rhipsalis)* 115, *170*, 188, *189*
    rat's tail *(Disocactus)* 188
    Saguaro 115
Calathea (peacock plant, rattlesnake plant) *24*, *26–7*, *161*, *180*, 184, 190, *205*
Cape primrose *(Streptocarpus)* *96*, 196
Capsicum (chilli pepper) *37*, *40–1*, 155, *194*
Carex (sedge) *76–7*
carnation (pink, *Dianthus*) 89, *94*, 95, *127*
carnivorous plant 80, *139*, 218, 221, 225
Celosia (cockscomb) *56*, *57*, *66–7*, *136*, 139
Cephalocereus 115
Cereus 115
Chamaedorea (parlour palm) 31, *178*
chamomile, yellow *(Anthemis tinctoria)* 72
chilli pepper *(Capsicum)* *37*, *40–1*, 155, *194*
chlorophyll 15, 17, 190
Chlorophytum comosum (spider plant) *103*, 174, *175*, *189*, 214
chrysanthemum (*Chrysanthemum x morifolium*) 72, *127*, 147, 155
Cleistocactus 166
cockscomb *(Celosia)* *56*, *57*, *66–7*, *136*, 139
compost 17, 21, 218, *220–1*, 226
container *124*, 126, *222–3*
Convallaria (lily-of-the-valley) 100, *149*, 159

cornfield 72
cowslip *(Primula veris)* 90
Crassula (jade plant) 113, *179*, *196*, *200*, *205*
crassulacean acid metabolism 117, 226
cuttings 232, *234–5*
Cyclamen (cyclamen) 89, *97*, *132*, *133*, *153*, *158*, 211
Cylindropuntia 115

Dahlia 57, *62–3*, 126, *127*, *134*, *137*
daffodil *(Narcissus)* *46–7*, *48*, 126, *139*, *147*, *153*, 155
daisies *72–3*, 126
    African *(Osteospermum)* *72–3*, *139*
    ox-eye *72–3*, *127*
    Michaelmas *(Aster x frikartii)* *72–3*
    painted *(Tanacetum coccineum)* *72–3*, *139*
    Shasta *(Leucanthemum x superbum)* *72–3*
dead-heading 231
devil's ivy *(Epipremnum aureum)* 31, *32–3*, *52*, *175*, *204*
Disocactus (rat's tail cactus) 188
dragon tree *(Dracaena)* *30–1*, *164*, *204*, *206*
dumb cane *(Dieffenbachiana)* *26–7*, *164*, *186*, 190

Echeveria (echeveria) *108*, *112–13*, *117*, *128*, *129*, *162*, 167, *182*, *183*, *202–3*
Echinocactus 166
Echinocereus 115
Echinopsis *108*, *114*, 115
elephant's ear *(Alocasia)* *26–7*, *174*, *185*, *204*
elephant's foot *(Beaucarnea*, ponytail palm) 31, *179*, *200*
epiphyte *28–9*, 53, *188–90*, 225
Epipremunum (devil's ivy, golden pothos) 31, *32–3*, *52*, *175*, *204*
Eschscholzia californica (Californian poppy) 73
Euphorbia (spurge) 115

fatsia 27, *128*, *129*
feeding 226
Felicia (blue marguerite) *72–3*, *139*
fern 45, *50–1*, *187*, 190, 225
    blue star *(Phlebodium)* 51, *190*, *191*
    Boston *(Nephrolepis)* 51, *175*
    button (*Pellaea*) *214*
    hart's tongue *(Asplenium)* *50*, 51, *143*, *210*
    maidenhair *(Adiantum)* *44*, 51, *103*, *175*, *186*, 190, *214*, *215*
    male (*Dryopteris*) 51, *128*
    painted *(Athyrium)* *128*
    shield *(Polysticum)* 51, *128*
fertiliser 220, 226
fescue, blue *(Festuca glauca)* *76–7*, 138, *139*
Festuca glauca (blue fescue) *76–7*, 138, *139*
Ficus elastica (rubber plant, rubber fig) *106*, *207*
flaming sword *(Vriesea splendens)* *28–9*, *197*, *205*
flamingo flower *(Anthurium)* *26–7*, 168, *169*, 196, 211
foliage care 228
forget-me-not *(Myosotis)* *74*, *91*, *142*, *143*
Fragaria x ananassa (strawberry) *34*, 35, *42*, *43*
frost 20
Fuchsia (fuchsia) *98*, 99, *102*, *132*, *133*, *137*, *142*, 147, 168, 230

Galanthus (snowdrop) *148*
golden pothos *(Epipremnum*, devil's ivy) 31, *32–3*, *52*, *175*, *204*

grass 69, *76–7*, *129*, *143*, *147*
    feathertop, fountain *(Pennisetum)* 77
    feather *(Nasella* or *Stipa)* 77, *139*, *147*
    Japanese forest *(Hakonechloa)* 14, 77
    pheasant's tail *(Anemanthele lessoniana)* 77, *128*, *139*
    silver *(Miscanthus sinensis)* 77, *127*
Guzmania lingulata (tufted air plant) *28–9*, *161*, *205*
Gymnocalycium 14, 115, *183*

Haworthia *108*, *116–17*, *168*, *184*, *203*
health 13–21, *220–1*, 224–31
heart-leaf plant *(Philodendron)* *32–3*, *161*, 168, *175*
heartsease *92–3*
hearts-on-a-string *(Ceropegia)* *174*
Helianthus (sunflower) *104–5*, 126, *127*, *136*
herbs 69, *70–1*, *139*, *194*, *195*, 235
Hibiscus rosa-sinensis (Chinese rose) *55*, *200*
Hippeastrum (hippeastrum) *46–7*, *201*
hosta (*Hosta*) *27*, *129*, *148*
houseleek *(Sempervivum)* *109*, *112–13*, *139*, 155
Howea (Kentia palm) *30–1*, *180*, *200*
Hoya (wax plant) 33, *177*, *204*
humidity 187–91, 193, 199, *204*, 225
Hyacinthus (hyacinth) *46–7*, *147*

Impatiens (busy Lizzie) 95, *137*, *143*, *159*, 231

jade plant *(Crassula)* 113, *179*, *196*, *200*, *205*
Japanese maple *(Acer palmatum)* 231
jasmine, indoor *(Jasminum)* 33, *110–1*, *117*, *164*, *173*, *204*

Kalanchoe (Flaming Katy) *183*, *210*, 211
Kentia palm *(Howea)* *30–1*, *180*, *200*

Lactuca (lettuce) 15, *34*, 35, *38*, *39*, *142*, 155, 168
lavender *(Lavandula)* *70–1*
leaf care 228
lemon balm *(Melissa)* *70–1*
lettuce *(Lactuca)* 15, *34*, 35, *38*, *39*, *142*, 155, 168
Lilium (lily) *46–7*, *128*, *129*, *140–1*
lily (*Lilium*) *46–7*, *128*, *129*, *140–1*
lily-of-the-valley *(Convallaria)* 100, *149*, 159
Lithops (living stone) *84–5*, 167, 168
living stone *(Lithops)* *84–5*, 167, 168
love-in-the-mist *(Nigella)* *68*, 73

maidenhair fern *(Adiantum)* *44*, 51, *103*, *175*, *186*, 190, *214*, *215*
Mammillaria *114–5*, *195*, *208*
marguerite *(Argyranthemum)* 72–3, *139*, 147
marjoram *(Origanum)* *70–1*
meadow *46*, 69, *72–3*, 76
Melica uniflora (wood melick) *76–7*, *143*
Melissa (lemon balm) *70–1*
Mentha (mint) *70–1*, *129*, *194*
mint (*Mentha*) *70–1*, *129*, *194*
misting leaves *175*, 228
Monstera (Swiss cheese plant) 99, *106–7*, 168, *204*, *205*, *206*, 230
moonstone *(Pachyphytum)* *85*, 167
moth orchid *(Phalaenopsis)* 45, *52–3*, *169*, *189*, *192*, 225
mother-in-law's-tongue *(Sansevieria)* *61*, 100, 101, *176*, *178*

Myosotis (forget-me-not) *74, 91,* 142, *143*

Narcissus (daffodil) *46–7, 48,* 126, 139, *147, 153,* 155
Nephrolepis (Boston fern) *50–1,* 175
Notocactus 115

Opuntia 115
orchid 45, *52–3, 169, 174, 189, 192,* 225
Origanum (marjoram) *70–1*
Osteospermum (African daisy) *72–3,* 139

Pachyphytum (moonstone) *85, 167*
palm *30–1, 178, 179*
    areca (*Dypsis*) *30–1,* 204, *206*
    Kentia (*Howea*) *30–1, 180,* 200
    parlour (*Chamaedorea*) *31, 178*
    ponytail (*Beaucarnea,* elephant's foot) *31, 179, 200*
pansy (*Viola*) *92–3*
Papaver (poppy) *68,* 73
peace lily (*Spathiphyllum*) 27, 196, *210*
peacock plant (*Calathea*) *24, 26–7, 161, 180, 184, 190, 205*
peat 80, *220–1*
peat-free compost 221
pelargonium 57, *60–1, 110–11, 133, 134, 150, 152, 153,* 155, *182,* 234
Pellaea (button fern) 214
peppermint (*Mentha*) 70, 129
Petunia 57, *64–5, 132, 133, 136,* 139, 159, 169
Phalaenopsis (moth orchid) 45, *52–3, 169, 189, 192,* 225
Philodendron 32–3, 161, 168, 175
photosynthesis 15, 114, 117, 190
Pilosocereus 115
pincushion flower (*Scabiosa,* scabious) *8,* 73, *138*
pink (carnation, *Dianthus*) 89, *94,* 95, *127*
pitcher plant (*Sarracenia*) 78, *80–1, 82*
plantain lily (*Hosta*) 27, 129, 148
pollination 41, 53, 188
polyanthus (*Primula*) 90, *91,* 142, *143,* 148, 158
ponytail palm (*Beaucarnea,* elephant's foot) *31, 179, 200*

poppy,
    field (*Papaver*) *68,* 73
    California (*Eschscholzia californica*) 73
pot-bound 227, 229
potting on 227
pricking out 233
primrose (*Primula*) 90, 149
Primula 90–1, *109–10,* 142, 148, *159*
    hybrid (auricula) *88, 158,* 159
    veris (cowslip) 90
    veris x vulgaris (polyanthus) 90, *91,* 148
    vulgaris (primrose) *90,* 149
problems 229
pruning 230–1

rat's tail cactus (*Disocactus*) 188
rattlesnake plant (*Calathea*) *24, 26–7, 161, 180, 184, 190, 205*
Rebutia 115
rose 45, *54–5, 127, 131, 211,* 230
    Chinese (*Hibiscus*) *55,* 200
rosemary (*Rosmarinus*) *70–1, 139, 194,* 234
rubber plant (rubber fig, *Ficus elastica*) *106, 207*

sage (*Salvia*) *70–1, 139,* 194
Saintpaulia (African violet) 89, *96, 196,* 214, 221, 228
Salvia (sage) *70–1*
Sansevieria (mother-in-law's-tongue) *61, 100,* 101, *176, 178*
Sarracenia (pitcher plant) 78, *80–1, 82*
Scabiosa (scabious, pincushion flower) *8,* 73, *138*
Sedum (stonecrop) *112–3, 154,* 155, *162, 167, 173, 182*
seed 231–3
seedling *169, 182, 231–3*
Sempervivum (houseleek) 109, *112–3, 139,* 155
Senecio rowleyanus (string-of-beads) *173*
snapdragon (*Antirrhinum*) *94,* 95
snowdrop (*Galanthus*) 148
Solanum lycopersicum (tomato) 35, *36,* 40–1, *126,* 139, 155
Spathiphyllum (peace lily) 27, 196, *210*
spider plant (*Chlorophytum*) 99, *103,* 174, *175, 189,* 214

spiderwort (*Tradescantia*) *103,* 174, *184,* 214
spurge (*Euphorbia*) 115
Stephanotis (bridal wreath) 33, *175,* 204
stonecrop (*Sedum*) *112–3, 154,* 155, *162, 167, 173, 182*
strawberry (*Fragaria*) *34, 42, 43*
Streptocarpus (Cape primrose) *96, 196*
string-of-beads (*Senecio rowleyanus*) *173*
succulent 112, 117, *129, 146, 154, 162, 166, 168, 173, 182, 184, 195, 202–3*
sunflower (*Helianthus*) *104–5,* 126, *127,* 136
Swiss cheese plant (*Monstera*) 99, *106–7,* 168, 204, *205, 228, 230*

thyme (*Thymus*) *70–1,* 139
Tillandsia (air plant) *86–7*
tomato (*Solanum lycopersicum*) 35, *36,* 40–1, *126,* 139, 155
top-dress 220
Tradescantia (spiderwort) *103,* 174, *184,* 214
Trichocereus 115
trouble-shooting 229
tufted air plant (*Guzmania*) *28–9, 161, 205*
Tulipa (tulip) *22,* 45, *46–7, 126, 130,* 139, *147,* 155

umbrella tree (*Schefflera*) 33
urn plant (*Aechmea*) *28–9, 205*

Viola (viola, pansy) 89, *92–3,* 155
Vriesea splendens (flaming sword) *28–9, 197, 205*

water butt 16, 124, 225
watering 224
wax plant (*Hoya*) 33, *177,* 204
wood melick (*Melica uniflora*) *76–7, 143*

Yucca (yucca) 179

Zamioculcas (Zanzibar gem, zee zee plant) 214, *215*

Acknowledgements

———

For wonderful plants: Royal Botanic Gardens, Kew; Joanne Everson, Squires Garden Centres

For brilliant i.d. skills: Paul Rees, Scott Taylor, Nick Johnson, Ginny Malmgren

For wonderful locations: Michael Benedito, Celia and Paul Coppock, Holly Hamill, Luke Montgomery Smith and Gina Geoghegan, Scott Taylor and Elisa Biondi, Phil King and Graham Clayton, Francine Raymond, Royal Botanic Gardens, Kew, Barbara and John at No 45, Linda at No 47, David at No 63, The Prince Albert in Twickenham, Percy Chapman's.

For wonderful body parts: Gina Geoghegan, Eoin Connelly Gorman, Holly Hamill, Harry the Hound, Eleanor Massey, Luke Montgomery Smith, Tom Pickering, Celso Robayo, Emma Turner

For wonderful pots: Catherine at No 43

For inspiration: Andreas Groeger